The Diary of James Hinton (1761–1823)

"Though reading this book will take a person about two hours, it will provide hours of reflection throughout a lifetime. Hinton's diary confronts a wide variety of spiritual concerns and reveals, among other things, a faithful pastor, a loving father, and a devoted husband. He was a man deeply in touch with his own soul, aware of the challenges to spiritual growth, the subtlety and ravages of indwelling sin, and the peculiar tendencies of his own temperament. He is also continually concerned about the effects of false teaching and his own struggles with 'unbelief' are noticeable in various portions of his diary. Such honesty, however, does not eclipse his sincere exultation in the riches of the person and work of Christ. His prayerful solicitation for God's providential graces in times of travel, family and personal sickness, and material provision also serve as a model for negotiating the uncertainties of this world with confidence and joyful hope. These reflections are a hidden treasure and will enrich all who discover it."

Tom J. Nettles, Senior Professor of Historical Theology, The Southern Baptist Theological Seminary

"All historians know the joy of finding buried treasure in the recesses of a dark library shelf. *The Diary of James Hinton* is one such treasure, as in these pages we find a man whose patient labors, deep biblical spirituality, and outgoing personality, all sparkle like gold. In the challenging times in which we live, I would encourage all pastors to feast on this treasure, especially during those dark days of ministry and life when it seems God has grown silent. Chance Faulkner has done the hard work of discovering Hinton's buried gems; it is now but for you to enjoy every facet of these Christ-saturated words to the benefit of your own soul."

Dustin W. Benge, Provost, Union School of Theology, Oxford, UK

"If I was allowed only one word to describe the man I have met in these pages it would be 'earnest.' These diary entries give us a window into the private life of a faithful pastor pressing on towards intimacy with God, even when he felt like he wasn't making much progress. His own description of his internal struggles have helped me further understand some of the things that go on in my own heart and for this I am grateful. This little book will be especially useful to pastors and will hopefully encourage them to keep going in the good fight of the faith, especially when under pressure."

Steve Auld, Pastor, Great Victoria Street Baptist Church, Belfast

"In *The Diary of James Hinton*, readers have the opportunity to witness the spiritual development of a pastor's heart. Despite the 200-year gap between Hinton's day and our own, his spiritual struggles should resonate with many pastors today as they represent an ordinary pastor wrestling with the many challenges of local church. I believe the church also stands in special need of Hinton's thoughts on the world's influence upon the heart and how they work to hinder a Christian's devotion to God. Though Hinton frequently expressed that it was 'more difficult to live Christ than to preach Christ,' we see in these pages that what had shaped him privately, he proclaimed publicly. Every pastor would be blessed to invest an hour or two to the reading of this diary for their own encouragement and an aid to personal devotion."

Stephen McKay, Adjunct Lecturer in Church History, Morling College, Sydney, Australia

"The temptation of many is to focus their studies only on the renowned figures of church history—the Luthers, the Calvins, the Edwardses, or the Spurgeons. Earnest students will obtain a more full-bodied understanding, however, as they also apply themselves to the less obvious facets of the gem of history. *The Diary of James Hinton* offers us a new window into the world of Andrew Fuller, John Ryland, Jr., and the Calvinistic Baptists of eighteenth-century Britain. While nothing remains of his original diary, James Hinton's thoughts have here been skillfully collected and reassembled to present a distillation of the heart and mind of a faithful English pastor. Anyone who is serious about Baptist history needs to own this volume. High marks to Chance Faulkner for this important work!"

Nate Pickowicz, Pastor, Harvest Bible Church, Gilmanton Iron Works, NH; Co-Author, *The American Puritans*

THE DIARY OF JAMES HINTON (1761-1823)

Introduced by MICHAEL A.G. HAYKIN

Edited by CHANCE FAULKNER

H&E Publishing

Published by: H&E Publishing, Peterborough, Ontario
www.hesedandemet.com

Source in Public Domain: John Howard Hinton, *A Biographical Portraiture of the late Rev. James Hinton, M.A.* (Oxford: Bartlett and Hinton/London: B. J. Holdsworth, 1824).

James Hinton (1761–1823) Pencil and charcoal drawing by Bethany Hacker, 2020 @jolie_.art

Paperback ISBN: 9781989174517
eBook ISBN: 9781989174524

First Edition, 2020

Contents

Preface ... ix
Chance Faulkner

Introduction ... 1
Michael A.G. Haykin

The Diary of James Hinton

1789 ... 16
1794 ... 17
1795 ... 20
1796 ... 26
1797 ... 31
1798 ... 32
1799 ... 42
1800 ... 47
1801 ... 57
1802 ... 60
1803 ... 65
1804 ... 67
1805 ... 69
1806 ... 70
1807 ... 72
1810 ... 73
1813 ... 75
1815 ... 76
1818 ... 77
1823 ... 78
Not dated ... 81
Appendix: Riot of Woodstock Narrative ... 83

PREFACE

Chance Faulkner

I first heard of James Hinton (1761–1823) while participating in an independent study on the eighteenth-century English Baptists with Dr. Michael A.G. Haykin at Toronto Baptist Seminary. During this study, I had the privilege of reading through Hinton's biography (*A Biographical Portraiture of the Late Rev. James Hinton*), written by his son, John Howard Hinton (1791–1873). What I read profoundly impacted and shaped me. Hinton was a man of loyal devotion to his family and a deep pastoral love for the people under his pastoral charge. He was also catholic in spirit—eager for relationships with those outside his tribe, and desiring, as he stated at his ordination in 1788, "to live in unity and peace with all that love our Lord Jesus Christ."[1] This desire for unity was a marvelous goal and a practice he was committed to until his final breath.

Hinton was someone who was suspicious of his own heart and regularly gave himself to self-examination. His diary is packed with remorse for his own shortcomings and indwelling sin, yet without despair, always looking towards the "cheerful hope" of the gospel, and the security and sufficiency of Christ's pardoning and redeeming mercy. Towards others he was generous, gracious, and always seeking to discern what was excellent in them, desiring to see their "character in the best possible light; never to see their failings, and even to think that they had none."[2]

---

[1] John Howard Hinton, *Biographical Portraiture of the Late Rev. James Hinton, M.A.* (Oxford: Bartlett and Hinton/London: B. J. Holdsworth, 1824), 106.

[2] Hinton, *Biographical Portraiture*, 287.

Hinton was a man of Christ-like piety. Sometimes the best mentors are those who have gone before us in previous generations—we can be sure they finished their race well. This is certainly true of James Hinton. His life and spirituality is a convicting example, worthy of careful study and imitation by all.

Editor's Notes

Because Hinton's original journal is not available, the following diary has been compiled from entries scattered throughout his biography.

Except for minor edits, this diary contains the text as originally published. Where the entry dates have not been supplied, I've suggested those that seem most probable.

As it is my hope that this little volume may prove helpful for others seeking to further study his life, I've also included footnotes noting where each diary entry can be found in *Biographical Portraiture.* I've also included some commentary in footnotes which will hopefully provide some context as to why certain entries were written. Included in the appendix is Hinton's account of the Woodstock Riot.

Acknowledgements

I am indebted to Dr. Michael Haykin, who agreed to write the excellent introductory essay to this work and assisted with the translation of Hinton's Latin phrases. It was Michael who first encouraged me to transcribe and compile this diary chronologically and I remain thankful for his friendship, counsel, and guidance throughout this project.

Chance Faulkner
Peterborough, ON
February 2020

James Hinton of Oxford: A biographical sketch

Michael A. G. Haykin

The name of the eighteenth-century Baptist minister James Hinton (1761–1823) is not one that is well-known by any standard, even to those who specialize in the study of English Baptist history. Yet, along with his friends Andrew Fuller (1754–1815) and John Ryland, Jr. (1753–1825), Hinton was "one of those Baptist leaders who, at the end of the eighteenth century, secured the revival of Baptist life in Britain."[1] And like many of his theological persuasion—Hinton

---

[1] J. H. Y. Briggs, "Hinton, John Howard" in *Oxford Dictionary of National Biography*, ed. H. C. G. Matthew and Brian Harrison (Oxford: Oxford University Press, 2004), 27:299. In his address at the interment of Hinton, Thomas Coles (1779–1840), of Bourton-on-the-Water, noted that the work of renewal of the Baptist denomination associated with the names of "a Carey, a Pearce, a Fuller, a Sutcliffe, a Ryland ... received the most cordial and effective co-operation in all their plans and exertions" from Hinton ("The Address Delivered at the Interment of the Late Rev. James Hinton of Oxford," *The Baptist Magazine*, 15 [1823]: 450).

For the biographical details about Hinton in this sketch, I am indebted to John Howard Hinton, *A Biographical Portraiture of the late Rev. James Hinton, M.A.* (Oxford: Bartlett and Hinton/London: B. J. Holdsworth, 1824); Edward Steane, "Personal Recollections," *The Sunday at Home* 20 (1873): 138–141; Philip Hayden, "The Baptists in Oxford 1656–1819," *The Baptist Quarterly*, 29 (1981-1982): 130–132; Raymond Brown, "'Fear God and honour the King': James Hinton and the Tatham Pamphlet Controversy" in Rosie Chadwick, ed., *A Protestant Catholic Church of Christ: Essays on the History and Life of New Road Baptist Church, Oxford* (Oxford: New Road Baptist Church, 2003), 107–135; and Tim Grass, "'Walking together in unity and peace and the fear of God': the Challenge of

was a Dissenter of Calvinistic Baptist convictions—Hinton regarded the keeping of a diary as a spiritual discipline. Hinton's diary is no longer extant, but large portions of it can be found embedded in a biographical study of Hinton by his son John Howard Hinton (1791–1873). This book contains these portions that have been skillfully re-assembled by Chance Faulkner as a diary. This introductory sketch of Hinton's life helps to set these diary extracts in their historical context.

"The beauty and suitableness of Christ as a Saviour"

James Hinton was raised in a solid Christian home. His father, Thomas Hinton (d.1787), was known to be a committed Christian in the town of Buckingham, Buckinghamshire, where he lived, and a man who had to endure petty acts of persecution throughout his life. One Saturday night, for example, the door knockers from quite a number of neighboring houses in Buckingham were wrenched from off their doors and somehow thrown into the front hall of his house. The people must have been told where they could retrieve their door knockers with the result that Hinton was bothered throughout that Lord's day—which he was in the habit of keeping as a day of rest—having to answer his door and find which door knocker belonged to whom.[2] Thomas Hinton's godly response to such attacks made a deep impression on his son James Hinton, who was converted in the mid-1770s. In the son's words, after severe mental wrestling with "deistical objections" to the Christian Faith, particularly, with regard to divine sovereignty, God brought him to the place where he saw "something of the beauty and suitableness of Christ as a Saviour for me, and enabled me to plead for his mercy, only on the ground of his satisfaction and death."[3]

In Hinton's early Christian experience, he derived much benefit from frequently hearing the preaching of the Anglican

---

Maintaining Ecumenical Ideals, 1780–1860" in Chadwick, ed., *Protestant Catholic Church*, 148–154.

[2] Hinton, *Biographical Portraiture*, 7–8.

[3] Hinton, *Biographical Portraiture*, 8–16. The quotes are from page 12.

Evangelical Thomas Scott (1747–1821) in a barn near Tingewick, not far from Buckingham.[4] From 1778 to 1783, Hinton served as an apprentice candle-maker in Chesham, Buckinghamshire, a town historically known for its four B's: boots, beer, brushes and Baptists![5] It was during this time as an apprentice that he developed, in the words of his son, John Howard Hinton, a remarkable "facility for meditating on divine things."[6] And it was also during his time at Chesham, he became convinced of believer's baptism by immersion. He was baptized on May 27, 1781, and joined the Baptist church in Chesham, whose origins dated back to the middle of the previous century.

The deacons of the Chesham church soon suggested that Hinton consider training for pastoral ministry, but it took Hinton nearly two years to agree. His father wrote a letter to Benjamin Beddome (1718–1795), the well-known pastor of the Baptist cause at Bourton-on-the-Water, to ask the principal of Bristol Baptist Academy, namely, Caleb Evans (1737–1791), for financial help for his son. And when Evans wrote back with "characteristic kindness, and ... assurance of considerable aid," Hinton's path was set.[7] In 1784 he began a three-year course of study at Bristol Baptist Academy, from 1784 to the spring of 1787. He treasured his years at Bristol, and was deeply convinced, in the words of his son and biographer that "though learning alone was worthless, it was of unspeakable value in association with piety."[8]

"Impossible to be in his company and be dull"

On June 1, 1787, Hinton went as a probationary minister to the open-communion, open-membership Baptist congregation in Oxford,

---

[4] Hinton, *Biographical Portraiture*, 14.

[5] George Piggin, *Tales of Old Chesham* (Beverley: Highgate Publications [Beverley], 1993), 21. For Piggin's brief discussion of the five Baptist churches in Chesham, see *Tales of Old Chesham*, 24–25.

[6] Hinton, *Biographical Portraiture*, 14.

[7] Hinton, *Biographical Portraiture*, 18–19.

[8] Hinton, *Biographical Portraiture*, 60. See also James Hinton, *The Union of Piety and Literature* (London, 1809).

now New Road Baptist Church in Bonn Square near the Westgate Centre. A Baptist congregation in Oxford had existed since at least 1653,[9] but by the close of the seventeenth century it was entering a state of decline, which lasted for much of the following century. Their church building was gutted during the Meeting-house riots of 1715, when upwards of fifty Nonconformists chapels were either destroyed or damaged by mobs hostile to Dissenters throughout England.[10] By the mid-eighteenth century, the church was without a pastor and in "a period of melancholy declension, during which assemblies for worship" rarely took place according to Hinton.[11] The cause was basically kept alive between the early 1740s and 1780 by a few men and women meeting for prayer on Sunday mornings and reading together sermons by John Owen (1616–1683) and other Puritan divines, though they did have preachers sometimes ride over from the Baptist cause at Bourton-on-the-Water.[12] Finally, in 1780 Daniel Turner (1710–1798), the pastor of the Baptist work in Abingdon, played a key role in helping re-establish the church on a the basis of a new covenant.[13] Two pastors, George Dyer (1755–1841), who later embraced Unitarianism, and Edward Prowitt, whose

---

[9] For the history of the congregation in the seventeenth century, see Roger Hayden, "'Through grace they are preserved': Oxford Baptists, 1640–1715" in Chadwick, ed., *Protestant Catholic Church*, 9–33.

[10] J. H. Y. Briggs, "Oxford and the Meeting-House Riots of 1715" in Chadwick, ed., *Protestant Catholic Church*, 35–64.

[11] James Hinton, *An Historical Sketch of Eighteen Baptist Churches, included in the Oxford Association, with Appropriate Reflections* (Oxford: I. T. Hinton, 1821), 6. See also Daniel Turner, *Charity the Bond of Perfection* (Oxford, 1780), iv.

[12] Turner, *Charity the Bond of Perfection*, iv; Hinton, *Historical Sketch of Eighteen Baptist Churches*, 6.

[13] See Paul S. Fiddes, "Receiving One Another: the History and Theology of the Church Covenant, 1780" in Chadwick, ed., *Protestant Catholic Church*, 65–105. For this covenant, see the Appendix.

ministry at Oxford was terminated in 1786 by heterodox views, preceded Hinton.[14]

The year after Prowitt's resigning the pastorate, the Oxford Baptists approached Caleb Evans for a recommendation as to a possible successor to Prowitt. Evans strongly suggested Joseph Kinghorn (1766–1832), who would later have a very distinguished ministry in Norwich and who was a fellow student and good friend of Hinton. But some of the Oxford congregation, having heard both Kinghorn and Hinton speak, considered Kinghorn "too deep ... for them," while Hinton seemed a "better speaker" and had a more "affable temper."[15] They thus called Hinton to supply the pulpit for six months, after which the church formally called him to be their pastor in January of 1788.[16] Not long after his call to Oxford, Hinton wrote to Evans and Kinghorn that the great thing he lacked in the church was "an intimate friend." Hinton went on to tell Evans and Kinghorn: "I love my people, but they are too busy on weekdays, and too pious on Sundays to form earthly friendships"![17] One cannot read the final clause of this remark without detecting a note of sarcasm.

Such a situation made Hinton all the more appreciative of close friendships with men like Samuel Pearce (1766–1799), whom

---

[14] On Dyer, see Ernest A. Payne, "The Baptist Connections of George Dyer," *The Baptist Quarterly*, 10 (1940–1941): 260–267 and Fiddes, "Receiving One Another: the History and Theology of the Church Covenant, 1780" in Chadwick, ed., *Protestant Catholic Church*, 93–96; on Prowitt, see Hinton, *Biographical Portraiture*, 104, and Hayden, "Baptists in Oxford 1656–1819," 130.

[15] Joseph Kinghorn, Letter to David and Elizabeth Kinghorn, April 2, 1787, in Martin Hood Wilkin, *Joseph Kinghorn of Norwich* (Norwich: Fletcher and Alexander, 1855), 108–109.

[16] Hinton, *Biographical Portraiture*, 18–24.

[17] James Hinton, Letter to Joseph Kinghorn and Caleb Evans, March 27, 1788 (3-page letter, privately owned).

Hinton had first met at Bristol.[18] In a letter that Pearce wrote to Hinton in the autumn of 1796, he told his Oxford friend:

> I embrace this opportunity to assure you of the sincere and heartfelt joy which the kind expressions of your friendship afford me, and of the reciprocal affection which my heart bears towards you. I am thankful for the providence which led me to an acquaintance with you: there are few with whom I feel such a congeniality of soul. O! it is the hope of heaven and its blest society, that best reconciles me to the distance at which we are now placed, and the consequent impossibility of frequent interviews.[19]

After Hinton's death, it was said of him that "it was impossible to be in his company and be dull."[20] Hinton was clearly an extrovert, who was energized by friends and company, for as his son noted, Hinton's "mind was strongly excited by society."[21] These qualities surely endeared him to Pearce. It should be noted that, from Hinton's perspective, Pearce was a model of holiness. Thus, writing to his son, he urged him to think about "Pearce and [Philip] Doddridge ... neither of them men of genius, but of great goodness, and diligence."[22]

Hinton was married in April of 1790 to Ann Taylor (1765–1832), a woman he once described as a "truly excellent

---

[18] Hinton, *Biographical Portraiture*, 95–96, 291. On Pearce, see Michael A.G. Haykin, *Joy unspeakable and full of glory: The piety of Samuel and Sarah Pearce* (Kitchener, ON: Joshua Press, 2012).

[19] Cited Hinton, *Biographical Portraiture*, 96.

[20] John Thomas Dobney, *The decease of eminent Ministers a source of Lamentation. A Sermon on the Death of the Rev. J. Hinton, A. M. Oxford* (Oxford: Munday and Slatter, 1823), 22.

[21] Hinton, *Biographical Portraiture*, 94.

[22] Hinton, *Biographical Portraiture*, 62.

companion."[23] Just over ten years after they were married, Hinton had the pleasure of baptizing Ann as a believer. As he noted in his diary:

> Her attendance on this ordinance, I rejoice to say, is a voluntary tribute to the dictates of conscience and the honour of Christ; and in this view I think highly indeed of her conduct. She had no motive of a domestic kind, for the affection of her husband was entirely hers; and his approbation too, as long as she saw not the command of Christ full and clear to direct her personal obedience. I bless God that not the least disaffection ... existed on account of this difference of opinion: and am particularly thankful, that I have never spoken one word that could induce her to think I should be more happy if she were a Baptist. The Lord has been her only teacher, and the throne of grace her only place of converse on this subject ...[24]

Hinton's Oxford congregation, it should be noted, was an open-communion, open-membership church.[25]

"Great solemnity ... with unction"

With next to no evangelical witness in Oxford, Hinton's early ministry in the town was, in the words of the Baptist historian Joseph Ivimey (1773–1834), in "one of the most difficult situations in which a Nonconformist minister in England could have been placed."[26] When Hinton was ordained in June of 1788, there were but twenty-

---

[23] Hinton, *Biographical Portraiture*, 50–51. The quote is from page 51 and was written on the eleventh anniversary of their marriage.

[24] Hinton, *Biographical Portraiture*, 74.

[25] For a criticism of the ecclesiology of Hinton, described as "the liberal and catholic Mr. Hinton," from the vantage-point of strict Baptist principles, see "Review: *A Biographical Portraiture of the late Rev. James Hinton, M. A.*," *The Baptist Magazine*, 16 (1824): 338–341.

[26] Joseph Ivimey, *The Excellence and Utility of an Evangelical Ministry, as exercised by Protestant Dissenters* (London: John Offor, 1823), A2.

five members, though the congregation included another hundred or so hearers.[27] Students at the University sought to disrupt the worship services from time to time and members of the congregation experienced significant difficulty in finding work in the town or sometimes found their businesses boycotted.[28] Hinton, however, was a gentle, caring pastor and thoughtful in his preaching. When Hinton preached on Sunday evenings, the majority of his congregation were increasingly not members of the church, but various Oxford residents along with a sizeable number of university students, some of whom came to merely ridicule the preacher and his preaching. Hinton, however, made a point of so constructing his evening sermons that while their wording gave no opportunity for mockery, they did not lack in pungency and power to smite the conscience. A good number of those who thus came to mock went away humbled, having come to respect Hinton, even though they did not respect his Baptist convictions. And there were some who were even converted. By the close of his ministry, the church's membership had grown to 270 and on a typical Sunday morning the congregation numbered around 800. A new building had been erected in 1798 (the core of the present church building), and further substantial enlargements made in 1819, four years before Hinton's death.[29]

A key part of the reason for the weight of Hinton's influence was his style of preaching: his sermons were methodical in their argument, perspicuous in language, and delivered with heart-felt eloquence. Edward Steane (1798–1882), the son of one of Hinton's

---

[27] Christina Colvin, "Protestant Nonconformity and Other Christian Bodies" in *A History of the County of Oxford: Volume 4, The City of Oxford*, ed. Alan Crossley and C. R. Elrington (London: Victoria County History, 1979), 418.

[28] Walter Stevens and Walter W. Bottoms, *The Baptists of New Road, Oxford* (Oxford, 1948), 12. Cf. also the remarks of Hinton, *Biographical Portraiture*, 107–108, 129–132.

[29] Hinton, *Biographical Portraiture*, 126–128, 132; Colvin, "Protestant Nonconformity and Other Christian Bodies," 418; "New Road Baptist Church Oxford: History" (http://newroad.org.uk/history/); Ivimey, *Excellence and Utility of an Evangelical Ministry*, 21.

deacons and later a prominent Baptist statesman and founder of the Evangelical Alliance, also recalled the impact of his public prayers. In Steane's recollection, Hinton's praying was ever a perfect blend of "great solemnity ... with unction" in which his intellect "was bathed in the profound humility and the tender, reverential love of the heart."[30]

Since the salary given to him by the church was not sufficient, Hinton also served as the headmaster of a small grammar school, which he started in 1791 with one student. Eventually the school came to number among its pupils some of the leading citizens of Oxford, a clear indication of the respect that Hinton came to enjoy, and came to be considered one of the most respectable private boarding schools in England.[31] But there were times when Hinton wrestled deeply with the way the school increased his worries and anxieties.[32] By April of 1795 he was praying for God "to open a way for the support of my family, with less concern in the world: I hope he will hear and grant my request."[33] But God did not see fit to grant this request, and Hinton eventually came to see that this was a key part of God's providential leading in his life. As he noted in a diary entry in 1815: "The school is often the sepulcher of devotion; but it enables me in many ways to serve the cause I love and live (I trust) to promote."[34]

Among his students were his own son John Howard and also Edward Steane, who remembered Hinton as a man of profound gravitas, whose dignity was punctuated by an impulsive generosity towards his students. He ever sought, Steane also remembered, to win their hearts to the "principles of a sound Scriptural morality

---

[30] Steane, "Personal Recollections," 138–139. I owe this reference to my research assistant and doctoral student, Baiyu A. Song.

[31] Steane, "Personal Recollections," 138; Hinton, *Biographical Portraiture*, 88.

[32] See the diary entries in Hinton, *Biographical Portraiture*, 89–90.

[33] James Hinton, Diary, entry for April 18, 1795, in Hinton, *Biographical Portraiture*, 90.

[34] James Hinton, Diary, entry for April 18, 1795, in Hinton, *Biographical Portraiture*, 90

and Evangelical religion."[35] Hinton later baptized Steane when he was around nineteen and discerning God's call on his life for gospel ministry, encouraged him to study at Bristol Baptist Academy, of which Hinton once noted: "Our denomination is clearly indebted (under God) more to that Academy than to any source of benefit besides."[36]

"Breeding civil mutiny and fomenting dissension"

Four years after his appointment as pastor of the New Road congregation, Hinton found himself embroiled in a pamphlet controversy with Edward Tatham (1749–1834), the Rector of Lincoln College, who had an extremely negative view of Dissenters.[37] In 1789, Tatham had given vent to his animus in the Bampton lectures, which were given annually before the university community. Tatham described Dissenting ministers as

> that formal and pompous class of men, ... who maintain, upon all occasions, the utmost solemnity of profession, and, on all subjects, the profoundest affectation of learning; whilst "the smell of Greek" has scarcely "passed upon their garments";—Instead of wasting their time in breeding civil mutiny and fomenting dissension in the state, if these superficial and ostensible, but industrious, men would make the Greek grammar the subject of their labours, the nation might be more free from faction for fifteen years to come.[38]

---

[35] E. B. Underhill, "Memorials of the Late Rev. Edward Steane, D. D.," *The Baptist Magazine*, 76 (1883): 1–2.

[36] Underhill, "Memorials of the Late Rev. Edward Steane," 3 and 4. The quotation from Hinton is on page 4.

[37] For this controversy, see especially Brown, "Fear God and honour the King" in Chadwick, ed., *Protestant Catholic Church*, 107–135.

[38] Edward Tatham, *The Chart and Sale of Truth, by which to find the Cause of Error* (Oxford, 1790), II, 116–117, note n.

Three years later, in 1792, Tatham followed up these acerbic remarks with an entire sermon devoted to an attack upon English Dissent, and in particular, Hinton and his Oxford congregation.

Basing his sermon on 1 John 4:1—an apostolic call to exercise doctrinal vigilance—Tatham contrasted the Anglican ministers trained at the state-supported divinity schools in the universities of Oxford and Cambridge with the "ignorant ... teachers of every [other] denomination, ... Methodists and Enthusiasts, ... Anabaptists and Dissenters." Such men were "self-taught without the power, and self-ordained without even the appearance, of learning ... Blind leaders of the blind." The Lincoln College Rector was adamant that these men were "artful and treacherous impostors" who were not only undermining the Church by their false doctrine but were also laboring to teach the English to despise the monarchy and so overturn the government and destroy the country in civil war "accompanied with horrors at which," he said, "our blood runs cold."[39] Tatham's patent dislike of Dissenters was rooted in a simplistic equation of rejection of Anglicanism with disloyalty to the British state.[40] Tatham was able to arrange to preach this sermon at five different parish churches in Oxford between November 18 and December 16, and the sermon proved to be so popular that it went through eight printings before the year's close.

Though a man whose temperament eschewed controversy, Hinton was convinced that something needed to be said in response to Tatham's scurrilous remarks. Hinton's *A Vindication of the Dissenters in Oxford, Addressed to the Inhabitants* went through four editions, and more than adequately answered the Tatham's charges. Hinton emphasized that Dissenters like himself were well "aware that learning is an excellent assistant in the ministry, though it

---

[39] Edward Tatham, *A Sermon Suitable to the Times* (London, 1792), 11, 13–15.

[40] Brown, "Fear God and honour the King" in Chadwick, ed., *Protestant Catholic Church*, 109.

cannot supersede the authority of Scripture."[41] He also rehearsed his own academic pedigree. He had "passed through the usual studies preparatory to the ministry in the Academy at Bristol" where he had studied under "worthy and well-known tutors," men like Caleb Evans and Robert Hall (1764–1831); and he had then been properly ordained with Evans, Samuel Stennett (1727–1795) of London and Daniel Turner (1710–1798) of Abingdon officiating at the ordination service.[42]

It bears noting that six years later, when France seemed to be poised for an invasion of England in the French Revolutionary Wars (1792–1802), Hinton published a small booklet in which he argued that their situation was one that could brook no neutrality. "Let us not desert our post," he urged his readers, "sully the glory of our ancestors, and willfully consign our sons to the disgraceful slavery of France."[43] To be sure, Hinton indicated, he prayed for peace; yet he was also convinced that a defensive war was not only just, but benevolent, for "it originates not in a desire to injure an enemy, but in a strong and virtuous impulse to protect our friends."[44] It was warmly commended by none other than Edward Tatham.[45]

---

[41] James Hinton, *A Vindication of the Dissenters in Oxford, Addressed to the Inhabitants* (4th ed.; London, 1792), 12.

[42] *Vindication of the Dissenters in Oxford*, 16–17. After describing briefly this course of study and his ordination, Hinton took the opportunity to express his regret that because he was not a member of any of the University colleges, he was "doomed to 'behold magnificent libraries' without the liberty of access to them" (*Vindication of the Dissenters in Oxford*, 21).

[43] James Hinton, *Brief Thoughts on the Importance of Defending our Country, Respectfully Addressed to the Inhabitants of Oxford and its Neighbourhood* (Oxford: R. Slatter, 1798), 3–4. I am indebted to Chance Faulkner for making a copy of this tract available to me.

[44] Hinton, *Brief Thoughts on the Importance of Defending our Country*, 11. See also his fascinating account of his visit to the battlefield of Waterloo exactly a month after that momentous battle in June, 1815: "A Visit to the Field of Battle at Waterloo," *The Baptist Magazine*, 7 (1815): 356–360.

[45] Hinton, *Biographical Portraiture*, 364–365; Brown, "Fear God and honour the King" in Chadwick, ed., *Protestant Catholic Church*, 127–129.

"No disgrace to our divine Master"

Hinton was also involved in preaching in a number of towns and villages surrounding Oxford, including Wheatley, Watlington, Littlemore, Oddington, and, most significantly, Woodstock.[46] In the spring of 1794 several inhabitants of Woodstock, who had heard Hinton preach in Oxford, approached him to see if he would be able to come to their town. They wanted him to speak to them in the home of Thomas Boulton in Oxford Street opposite the Marlborough Arms Inn. It was arranged that Hinton would come to the town on the evening of Sunday, May 18. But no sooner had Hinton begun to speak on the Scriptures that evening than a mob of some 300 or 400 surrounded the house and with extreme violence compelled Hinton to end the meeting. Hinton later wrote in his diary when got home to Oxford the evening of May 18:

> A dreadful riot at Woodstock this day: myself, and four companions, much wounded by the mob, with difficulty escaped with our lives. Blessed be God, who did not leave us in the hands of the enemy! ... May the great God so ordain, that this persecution may be the commencement of much good to the numerous inhabitants of Woodstock! My mind is very happy, thinking it an honour that I am accounted worthy to bear in my body the marks of the Lord Jesus, and to suffer for his name.[47]

---

[46] Hinton, *Biographical Portraiture*, 251–285; Stevens and Bottoms, *Baptists of New Road, Oxford*, 13–15.

[47] Hinton, *Biographical Portraiture*, 261. For the full account of the Woodstock Riot, see Hinton, *Biographical Portraiture*, 255–263. See also Michael A.G. Haykin, *"Accounted Worthy to Bear in my Body the Marks of the Lord Jesus": James Hinton, the Persecution of English Dissent, and the Woodstock Riot*, Occasional Publications [of the Andrew Fuller Center for Baptist Studies], no. 8 (Louisville, KY: The Andrew Fuller Center for Baptist Studies, 2018). This account is also available as an appendix in this volume.

In the aftermath of the Woodstock Riot, numerous individuals in Oxford who had once been friendly to Hinton would have nothing to do with him and shunned his company. They obviously thought that the Baptists were somehow at fault for the riot. Others even went so far as to curse Hinton to his face in the street and tell him that they wished he had been killed in the riot.[48] But Hinton was not to be deterred. He continued to defend village preaching, identical to what was attempted at Woodstock, since what he called "the great commission of Christ to his ministers is still in force, 'Go preach the gospel to every creature.'"[49] Moreover, Hinton believed he not only had a dominical command, but also divine example, for "to preach ... in any convenient place, to any person, and to all who would hear him, was surely no disgrace to our divine Master."[50] Given such a mindset, it is not surprising that Hinton was closely associated with Andrew Fuller and John Ryland in their leadership of the Baptist Missionary Society.[51] Hinton had the joy of seeing a church planted in Woodstock in 1819.[52]

---

[48] Hinton, *Biographical Portraiture*, 266–267.

[49] Hinton, *Biographical Portraiture*, 267.

[50] Hinton, *Biographical Portraiture*, 269.

[51] Hinton, *Biographical Portraiture*, 312–320. See also "An Abridgment of Mr. Hinton's Missionary Sermon preached at Spa-Fields Chapel, June 21, 1815," *The Baptist Magazine*, 7 (1815): 406–413, in which Hinton registered his deep admiration of the way that Fuller's "ardour of soul approaching to sacred enthusiasm" was "combined with a coolness and prudence which could weigh a multiplicity of jarring circumstances in the nicest balance" and that could inspire "our hearts with love" ("Abridgment of Mr. Hinton's Missionary Sermon," 411). Preached only three days after the Battle of Waterloo, Hinton's sermon made free use of martial imagery to drive home to himself and his hearers their responsibility to continue Fuller's missionary labors: "Fuller fell—gloriously fell in the arms of victory. He fell, giving directions to his fellow-soldiers to continue the conflict; assuring them that they also should share his triumph. How great is our responsibility who received the charge from his hands!" ("Abridgment of Mr. Hinton's Missionary Sermon," 412).

[52] Hinton, *Biographical Portraiture*, 278–279; "Ordinations, etc.," *The Baptist Magazine*, 19 (1827): 234.

Coda

I, for one, am deeply thankful for the time that Chance Faulkner has devoted in assembling what remains of Hinton's diary, and helping to make available an important witness to Baptist life and piety in that most momentous of eras in Baptist history, namely, the long eighteenth century.

1789

I bless God for a heart to pity the fatherless and receive the orphan.[1]

[1] James' brother, Thomas Hinton (1760–1789), died leaving his wife, Ann, and two children behind. One of Hinton's nephews was taken out of the Orphan School of London, but because of finances Hinton was not able to take both of them. See John Howard Hinton, *A Biographical Portraiture of the late Rev. James Hinton, M.A.* (Oxford: Bartlett and Hinton/London: B. J. Holdsworth, 1824), 72–73. However, Hinton's diary entry on April 23, 1799 states, "committing to his kind providence and richer grace the children he hath given us, as well as the dear *orphans* ..." By this time, eleven years from this 1789 entry, it seems Hinton had acquired both of the children (emphasis my own).

1794

January 17, 1794 [Friday][1]
On the whole a comfortable journey; and, considering the hurry of the world, I have enjoyed much communion with God.

February 7, 1794 [Friday][2]
Assisted much in study: blessed be God, who considers my many hinderances, and makes my strength equal to my day.

February 8, 1794 [Saturday][3]
Encouraged to bring new sermons into the pulpit, though I have but a short time to study them. A very happy day. In the evening my spirit filled with serious awe of eternal things: text, "Behold he cometh with clouds."[4]

April 19, 1794 [Saturday][5]
On the whole rather low and uncomfortable in mind, though not without a mixture of cheerful hope.

April 23, 1794. Fourth wedding day [Wednesday][6]
Committed myself in company with my dear wife to him, who has hitherto made this union truly happy.

---

[1] Hinton, *Biographical Portraiture*, 91.

[2] Hinton, *Biographical Portraiture*, 112.

[3] Hinton, *Biographical Portraiture*, 112.

[4] Revelation 1:7.

[5] Hinton, *Biographical Portraiture*, 26.

[6] Hinton married Anne (Taylor) Hinton (1766–1832) on April 23, 1790. *Biographical Portraiture*, 51.

May 18, 1794 [Sunday][7]
A dreadful riot at Woodstock this day: myself, and four companions, much wounded by the mob, with difficulty escaped with our lives.[8] Blessed be God, who did not leave us in the hands of the enemy! May the blood of a good man, shed this day in the streets of that unhappy town, not cry to heaven for vengeance! rather let us pray, "Father forgive them: lay not this sin to their charge"[9] May the great God so ordain, that this persecution may be the commencement of much good to the numerous inhabitants of Woodstock! My mind is very happy, thinking it an honour that I am accounted worthy to bear in my body the marks of the Lord Jesus, and to suffer for his name.

May 30/31, 1794 [Friday/Saturday][10]
A happy, though a trying week. Pleasant meditations. It is good for me to be thus afflicted; yea, "all things work together for good."[11]

July, 1794[12]
Very calm and happy. Enabled to leave the church (which some attempt to disturb) and my ministry (which some much despise) in the hands of a merciful and covenant keeping God. He is never cruel but ever kind. Accept my poor services, and pardon all my faults.

---

[7] Hinton, *Biographical Portraiture*, 261.

[8] For Hinton's account of this event see appendix. See also, Michael A.G. Haykin, *"Accounted Worthy to Bear in my Body the Marks of the Lord Jesus": James Hinton, the Persecution of English Dissent, and the Woodstock Riot*, Occasional Publications [of the Andrew Fuller Center for Baptist Studies], no. 8 (Louisville, KY: The Andrew Fuller Center for Baptist Studies, 2018).

[9] Luke 23:34; Acts 7:60.

[10] Hinton, *Biographical Portraiture*, 262.

[11] Romans 8:28.

[12] Hinton, *Biographical Portraiture*, 144.

August 8, 1794 [Friday][13]
Subjects for thankfulness: the little impression made on the harmony of the church by some attempts to disturb it. Yet there is danger, and I commit my dear people to Israel's keeper; determining, by grace, not to be surprised or cast down, though some of them should deal unkindly.

August 16, 1794 [Saturday][14]
Have redeemed too little time for prayer this week: O Lord, forgive me!

August 23, 1794 [Saturday][15]
A calm, comfortable, and spiritual week; blessed be God.

October 25, 1794 [Saturday][16]
A good week. I hope corruption has been kept low, though I have many struggles in my heart.

November 29, 1794 [Saturday][17]
Very hard pressed for time by cares and a multiplicity of concerns; yet more comfortable than I could expect.

December 13, 1794 [Saturday][18]
Very comfortable in thinking on "the unsearchable riches of Christ:"[19] great liberty of thought; blessed be God for affording it.

---

[13] Hinton, *Biographical Portraiture*, 144.
[14] Hinton, *Biographical Portraiture*, 26.
[15] Hinton, *Biographical Portraiture*, 26.
[16] Hinton, *Biographical Portraiture*, 26.
[17] Hinton, *Biographical Portraiture*, 26.
[18] Hinton, *Biographical Portraiture*, 112.
[19] Ephesians 3:8.

1795

January 1, 1795 [Thursday][1]
The last year, on the whole, was as full of trials as any past one, and I believe more full of spiritual comforts than any I have yet spent: blessed be God for both. My chief delight, a lively sense of divine things on my mind, and an increasing confidence of my gracious pardon and acceptance in the Beloved.

January 9, 1795 [Friday][2]
The Searcher of hearts knows, I trust, that I have given her sincerely to him. A very merciful day; may it not be soon forgotten.[3]

January 21, 1795 [Wednesday][4]
Began school, I hope under the smiles of heaven; but too much business robs me of my spiritual comfort.

February 7, 1795 [Saturday][5]
A comfortable week, though sin attempts again to reign. Lord help me to crucify it!

---

[1] Hinton, *Biographical Portraiture*, 26.

[2] Hinton, *Biographical Portraiture*, 52.

[3] On the birth of, Ann (Hinton) Bartlett (1795–1865), his first daughter. I am indebted to Melody (Dunn) Young who helped me come into possession of her register of birth and final will.

[4] Hinton, *Biographical Portraiture*, 89.

[5] Hinton, *Biographical Portraiture*, 26.

February 27, 1795 [Friday][6]
"Be clothed with humility":[7] considering the barren state of my heart, I ought to be so.

February 28, 1795 [Sunday][8]
Reason to be thankful for some little revivals. O Lord prevent coldness of heart from returning.

March 14, 1795 [Saturday][9]
This has been, I hope, a week of some spiritual improvement: God grant that it may be the earnest of still greater measures of it!

April 17, 1795 [Friday][10]
Some attacks of infidelity; may God remove them by the light of his countenance. I fear not to examine the truths of religion, but God alone can give me that evidence which arises from the power of them on the heart.

April 18, 1795 [Saturday][11]
A happy week, though with some sad exceptions from worldly-mindedness and distracting thoughts. My great hinderance in the divine life is an anxiety about worldly things, with a backwardness to secret prayer, and a want of spirituality in my mind; yet I hope I may bless God for some times of refreshing, and some successful struggles against these, alas! too common evils ... I have been earnest with God to open a way for the support of my family, with less concern in the world: I hope he will hear and grant my request.

---

[6] Hinton, *Biographical Portraiture*, 26.
[7] 1 Peter 5:5.
[8] Hinton, *Biographical Portraiture*, 26.
[9] Hinton, *Biographical Portraiture*, 26.
[10] Hinton, *Biographical Portraiture*, 27.
[11] Hinton, *Biographical Portraiture*, 27, 90.

June 13, 1795 [Saturday][12]

Having this day an opportunity I seldom enjoy, I have been in the presence of God, reviewing my past life for seven or eight weeks. I find that I have—through a great pressure of family cares, and constant engagement in the school, in visiting and in public labours, and above all, through a culpable negligence which has its source in aversion to God and devotion—but too much reason to use the language of Solomon, "They made me keeper of the vineyards, but mine own vineyard have I not kept."[13] I do indeed struggle against this carelessness and confusion of mind, and pray God to give me strength to walk more closely with him. I hope I can from my heart say I love to be employed in his work, and regret a want of time for retirement. I have endeavoured to obtain it early in the morning, but find the practice injures my health. I have not sufficient resolution to snatch half an hour from reading or company, and heart-examination is neglected. I pity and pray for the people of God who are overwhelmed with cares. I desire sincerely to repent, and to commence again from this day a more close walk with God: I trust in his pardoning mercy to cancel, my past guilt, and to give me strength for the future; and I present these resolutions and petitions to him in the name of the Lord Jesus Christ.

July 24, 1795 [Friday][14]

I hope I am recovering from the effects of over anxious cares. I trust some disappointments have been sanctified; God grant they may be more so! The anxiety of settling the half-year's account, and the fear lest my temporal concerns should not prosper and my family be supported, has been too much on my mind; and I have not committed it to God as I ought: I desire to be humble on this account; it has brought leanness into my soul. Lord, forgive the sin, and remove both cause and effect! I feel happy in returning to my rest, and find

---

[12] Hinton, *Biographical Portraiture*, 27.

[13] Song of Songs 1:6.

[14] Hinton, *Biographical Portraiture*, 89–90.

something of the sweetness of that text, "Casting all your care upon him, for he careth for you."[15]

August 8, 1795 [Saturday][16]

I hope I may say, as in the sight of God, I desire—may I not without presumption say, I believe God has given me—some increase of piety, spirituality, and calmness. Yet, Lord, how low are the graces of the Spirit, and what crowds of cares, as well as dulness of mind, prevent my communion with thee! Circumstances in the nation, in my family, and all around me, teach me a lesson which I have need to learn—"Seek not high things for thyself."[17] God is merciful to check a heart too fond of forming schemes for being happy in a state that is not my rest.

October 25, 1795 [Sunday][18]

Have been encouraged to labour more in preparing my evening sermons: O may God render them abundantly useful to the multitudes who attend!

November 7, 1795 [Saturday][19]

The past week or two, dull in my mind; the Lord hides his face. On examination, I find I have been worldly, languid in secret prayer, and too negligent: let me humble myself, and return to the Lord. O what a heart have I! I feel that I am not able to think a good thought. Yet I have some comfort left: blessed be God, the throne of grace is open, and I feel, amidst many engagements, a desire to redeem more time for the Lord; O may he strengthen my weak resolution, and give me to live more near to him.

---

[15] 1 Peter 5:7.

[16] Hinton, *Biographical Portraiture*, 28.

[17] Jeremiah 45:5.

[18] Hinton, *Biographical Portraiture*, 112.

[19] Hinton, *Biographical Portraiture*, 28.

November 28, 1795 [Saturday][20]
I condemn myself before God for an earthly mind, and a heart too much perplexed. I thank God for support, but do not find the increase in the divine life that I wish. I do not enough keep under corrupt passions: I do not bring them into subjection, but they bring me into temptation. Yet I dare not think of resigning the conflict; on the contrary, I would in divine strength put on afresh the armour of the gospel.

... Forever blessed be the God of my life, the Father of my spirit, for his patience with, and his kindness to, an unworthy worm through the past year. I am surprised at his kindness and my ingratitude. If I measure improvement by real sanctification rather than by comfort, I fear the account is worse than it here stands; but the blood of Christ cleanseth from all sin.[21] I hope I am not gone back. I hope I can discover some growth in grace. My chief fears are grounded on the existence, and too often something like an indulgence, of easy besetting sins. My chief evidences are a delight in communion with God in private as well as public, a willingness to resign my own will and all my interests to his control, and a hope that my besetting sins have on the whole been more crucified, and the path of duty more delightful. But how little the progress, how many the imperfections and sins of the past year! What could comfort, were it not that the Lord delighteth in mercy, and waiteth to be gracious! Lord, I would solemnly this day set out afresh for heaven, and once more resign myself and all I have to thee, through Jesus Christ: accept me through him. Amen.

1795 on the Sickness of Ann[22]
Mrs. H[inton] very ill this week: it makes me very gloomy, but let me hope in the Lord, he is yet gracious.

---

[20] Hinton, *Biographical Portraiture*, 28–29.
[21] 1 John 1:7.
[22] Hinton, *Biographical Portraiture*, 73.

Over anxious today; yet enabled to carry all, with my dear partner, to the throne of a faithful God.

I thank God for resignation during the illness of my wife, and I trust the affliction has been sanctified to us both. O God, if it please thee, remove it; but prepare me for thy will!

1796

January 23, 1796 [Saturday][1]

Favoured, I trust, with much communion with God: and, after much anxiety and fear lest I should think or act wrong, especially with regard to the great question of removing from Oxford,[2] which lies very heavy on my mind, I have (blessed be God) found great liberty and sweetness in committing this concern to his hands, with what may be (as far as human creatures can do anything perfect) a perfect resignation to his will, and making his glory my great and sole aim.

March 27, 1796 [Sunday][3]

At the end of this sermon I delivered to my people my determination to continue my labours among them, which was received with much pleasure. This important affair has much occupied my mind for three months. I remark respecting it—

1. That the idea of a removal was by no means my own seeking, not even in the most indirect manner.

2. That God enabled me from the first to hold my mind open to every intimation of his will, and made me sincerely, and above all things, desirous to know how and where I might most effectually promote his glory.

3. That he has graciously answered my prayer, by making it plainly appear to be my duty to remain at Oxford, and by uniting me to my people, and them to me, in closer bonds of affection than ever.

---

[1] Hinton, *Biographical Portraiture*, 150.

[2] In the fall of 1795, Samuel Stennett (1727–1795), the pastor of Little Wild Street Church in London died, and Hinton was asked if he would consider the call to be the church's new pastor. See Hinton, *Biographical Portraiture*, 145.

[3] Hinton, *Biographical Portraiture*, 153.

May 21, 1796 [Saturday][4]
Have enjoyed some very pleasant seasons, especially on Sabbath evenings. My faith has been somewhat shaken, or the vigour of it lessened, by doubts lest the foundation should fail. I have passed some strong conflicts with an easy besetting sin, and I trust God has given me to overcome by the blood of the Lamb; I record this to his praise. I beseech thee, O Lord, never leave me nor forsake me! I condemn myself for negligence, and lament my weakness, in the closet. I desire to approach the cleansing fountain, to renew a sense of pardon, and receive an increase of strength. But, Lord help me, or I shall lose the race.

June 7, 1796 [Tuesday][5]
To the young—"I thy servant fear the Lord from my youth."[6] I desire humbly to thank God for a considerable portion of his presence. Lord, keep me humble; let my comforts sanctify me, and do thou increase them a thousand-fold.

June 9, 1796 [Thursday][7]
This has been a truly pleasant day; blessed, blessed, blessed be God: O may its divine influence be permanent! A large congregation in the morning, and I was much affected in addressing them: Lord, affect their hearts, and turn them from the error of their ways unto thyself. "We long to see thy churches full."

---

[4] Hinton, *Biographical Portraiture*, 29–30.
[5] Hinton, *Biographical Portraiture*, 113.
[6] 1 Kings 18:12.
[7] Hinton, *Biographical Portraiture*, 113.

End of May, 1796[8]

This has been election week ... I have learnt that the honour of men is little to be trusted. I have felt that it is hard to be steadfast against the frowns and the smiles of superiors. I have above all found that much intercourse with the world is unfriendly to the health of the soul, and I long for returning tranquility.

August 20, 1796 [Saturday][9]

On a review of a few weeks past, my experience has been various—some very very happy, and some very dull days. Saturday evenings and Sabbath mornings generally happy. The world has too much influence on my heart, yet I thank God it does not produce an entire forgetfulness of religion. Faith is often shaken, but does not let go its hold. Sometimes my evening walks in the fields are truly delightful, and I hope I am indulged with real communion with God; but ah! how short the pleasing scene!

September 3, 1796 [Saturday][10]

I this day enter on my thirty-sixth year. Half the three score and ten I have lived; how unlikely I shall live the other half! I fear I am but little fitted to die; yet I think I believe in and love the Saviour, approve his gospel, and long to be like him—and were it not for indwelling sin, I should be a very happy man. I hope sin does not reign; and I hope, through grace, to arrive at the place where it does not exist.

---

[8] The election was between Henry Peters (*c.* 1763–1827) (658 votes), Francis Burton (d.1832) (504 votes), and Athur Annesley (1760–1841) (461 votes), and took place from May 23–27, 1796. See Henry Stooks Smith, *The Parliaments of England from 1st George I to the present tim*e (London: Simpkin, Marshall, & Co., 1845), II, 5; see also http://www.historyofparliamentonline.org/volume/1790-1820/constituencies/oxford (accessed February 13, 2020).

[9] Hinton, *Biographical Portraiture*, 30.

[10] Hinton, *Biographical Portraiture*, 30.

September 12, 1796 [Monday][11]
Today I feel the burden too heavy: my soul is dark, and family cares are too much multiplied. Yet I hope I am in the path of duty, and in the exercise of cheerful gratitude; but ashamed I am so fretful.

October 10, 1796 [Monday][12]
Blessed be God for this mercy! I mourn that my heart is not more affected with it: but my passions are strange things, hardly ever what they ought to be—too much moved, or too much unmoved. I hope I have sincerely given her to God.[13]

November 27, 1796 [Sunday][14]
My soul is not very prosperous: I hope to make it a matter of humiliation and prayer to God, that if I have piety it may be revived, and if not, that I may yet be converted. Lord hear me, for the Redeemer's sake. Amen.

Self-Examination. Have I ever experienced a total change of views, desires, affections, pursuits, and expectations? O Lord, thou knowest (I trust) that I have. In most things it appears clear, but in some still doubtful. Why not more clear? Some neglect occasions it—and my conflict with easy besetting sins, when it seems likely to be crowned with victory, is impeded, 1. by darkness of soul bordering on total unbelief; or, 2. by such hesitation as takes away the power of spiritual delight and improvement; or, 3. by a sudden return of the sin in its power, though I hope its returns are less strong. Am I truly humble for my neglect of secret duty and my carnal-mindedness? I trust I am in a measure: Lord humble me more, and give me more decided victory! Look down O Lord! My hope is in thee, and with all the faith I have, I hang on thine arm.

---

[11] Hinton, *Biographical Portraiture*, 90.
[12] Hinton, *Biographical Portraiture*, 52.
[13] In reference to the birth of his second daughter, Sarah (1796–1813).
[14] Hinton, *Biographical Portraiture*, 30–31.

December 3, 1796 [Saturday][15]
Examination for the Lord's Supper. Have I knowledge to discern the Lord's body? I hope God has given it to me, so far as relates to the understanding; but oh, how inefficacious! Have I repentance? I hope that I hate sin, and that I do by no means habitually indulge it: I hope I more and more hate that which most easily besets me, but I want a contrite and a broken heart; Lord give it me! Have I love? I hope I have; but oh, how weak. Have I faith to feed upon Christ? This too is weak, though he is my only dependence, and I dare trust no other. Have I new obedience? Ah! here I am ashamed; yet "seek thy servant O Lord, for I do not forget thy testimonies."[16] "To me belong shame and confusion of face, but to thee belong tender mercy and forgiveness."[17] Amen.

---

[15] Hinton, *Biographical Portraiture*, 31.

[16] Psalm 119:176.

[17] Richard Allestree, *The Whole Duty of Man: Laid Down in a Plain and Familiar Way for the Use of All, But Especially the Meanest Reader* (London: W. Norton, 1704), 455.

1797

February 16, 1797 [Thursday][1]

Spent this evening pleasantly in visiting the poor of the flock.

October 7, 1797 [Saturday][2]

Not so spiritual in mind as I ought to be, owing I fear to neglect of private prayer and meditation. Too much prone to anger, which is my besetting sin; Lord help me to lay it aside: I suffer myself to be diverted from the closet: Lord, I here make my humble confession that I do not redeem time as I ought, that I give it too easily to trifles. I do not in the course of the day think on God as I ought, nor exercise ejaculatory prayer. I pray for the application of the blood of Christ, and a thorough reform in the spirit of my mind, and in the temper and conduct of my life. O Lord, aid by thy grace a poor feeble worm!

After prayer. I bless God that he has given me some liberty to plead with him, and I go from his presence refreshed. O God, let me be watchful against the return of sin, and be thou my guard.

---

[1] Hinton, *Biographical Portraiture*, 199.

[2] Hinton, *Biographical Portraiture*, 31–32.

1798

August 16, 1798 [Thursday][1]

The new meeting-house opened. A prayer meeting in the vestry from seven till nine in the morning: a very happy season, and an anticipation, I trust, of many more. Public service at eleven: preachers Mr. Hughes[2]—"Will God in very deed dwell with man on the earth"—and Dr. Ryland[3]—"I will glorify the house of my glory." Public service again at six in the evening; preacher Mr. Cooke[4]—"I never said to the seed of Jacob, Seek ye me in vain."[5] All very excellent sermons, and uncommon life and cheerfulness of spirit seemed to pervade the assembly. I do indeed hope the Lord was with us of a truth.

---

[1] Hinton, *Biographical Portraiture*, 157–158.

[2] Joseph Hughes (1769–1833) was an English Baptist minister in Thameside Village. He played a vital role in the formation of the British Foreign Bible Society, and was secretary of the Religious Tract Society. See "Hughes, Joseph," in *Dictionary of Evangelical Biography (1730–1866)*, ed. Donald M. Lewis (Peabody, MS: Hendrickson, 2004), 1:580.

[3] John Ryland Jr. (1753–1825) was an English Baptist minister and theologian. In 1781 he was ordained at the age of seventeen and co-pastored in Northampton with his father John Collet Ryland (1723–1792). Ryland played a vital role in the formation and administration of the Baptist Missionary Society. After the death of Andrew Fuller (1754–1815), Ryland became joint secretary with James Hinton. Unfortunately, because of health issues, Hinton was only joint secretary for one year (1816–1817). On Ryland, see "Ryland, John," *Dictionary of Evangelical Biography 1730–1860*, 2:965–966; on Hinton as secretary, see Hinton, *Biographical Portraiture*, 317–321.

[4] At this point Mr. Cooke has not been identified.

[5] Isaiah 45:19.

August 22, 1798 [Wednesday][6]
Enabled to redeem some time for the closet, but not so happy in prayer as I could wish. Calm in my temper—I hope some improvement. Did not redeem so much time for evening prayer as I ought; and yet, being at a meeting for Sunday-schools, it is very difficult to know what is really my duty.

August 24, 1798 [Friday][7]
Comfortable in morning devotion, and diligent in business through the day. Found my mind hurt, that is, unfitted for devotion, by reading Shakespeare's "All's well that ends well."[8] Could not recover a good frame for prayer-meeting, was obliged to fly to the well-known blessed fountain that is open for guilt: blessed be God it is still open!

August 25, 1798 [Saturday][9]
Saturday. I hope I am sincerely and earnestly desirous of the divine presence to day.

Evening. My desire has been granted. I have had considerable pleasure in studying the subjects for tomorrow; yet I lament the poverty of my mind in devotion, and its feebleness and contractedness in regard to the fulness of divine truth. If a child of God, what a babe am I in knowledge and experience!

August 26, 1798 [Sunday][10]
Preached today from Eph. iii. 19. "That ye might be filled with all the fulness of God." A great subject: my mind much interested, and very happy in my discourse. Afternoon, from Heb. iv. 2. "The word preached did not profit": I hope feeling its importance, and delivering the word with much freedom. At Wheatley, from Rom. ii. 4.

---

[6] Hinton, *Biographical Portraiture*, 32.

[7] Hinton, *Biographical Portraiture*, 32.

[8] William Shakespeare's famous play "All's well that ends well" was first published in 1623.

[9] Hinton, *Biographical Portraiture*, 113.

[10] Hinton, *Biographical Portraiture*, 113.

"The goodness of God leadeth thee to repentance." Here also I felt my mind very earnest: the congregation was large, and the people attentive ... O may God fix his word upon their hearts, and honour his name by their conversion! The day truly pleasant: blessed be God. O may I live so as to prove my own sincerity, and exemplify the power of the doctrine I have taught!

August 30, 1798 [Thursday][11]
Visited—, at Hinksey; and see the necessity that the flock were oftener visited, to admonish and stir them up to duty.

August 31, 1798 [Friday][12]
Have greatly to complain of a want of the presence of God in secret devotion, though much enlarged at prayer meeting.

September 3, 1798 [Monday][13]
This day I enter into my 38th year. How important the day of my birth!—much more important will be the day of my death. The greater part of my life is in all probability gone, and when I look back on the year I have spent, I am covered with shame and confusion to think how little I have done for God, and how little my own character has been improved. Twenty-six years I have been ranked among the professors of experimental religion, and about twenty years in the constant habit of communing with the people of the Lord at his table. Ah, how little have I crucified the flesh with its affections and lusts. How little have I adorned the doctrine of God my Saviour! I hope I have some evidences that I am a child of God, but too many dark signs appear: grovelling affections, too great a regard to human applause, a deadness in secret devotion, a want of spirituality in my converse, a want of love for souls, a want of due care to improve precious time—these are among my chief enemies, to oppose whom I desire again to put on the gospel armour, and begin this day with a

[11] Hinton, *Biographical Portraiture*, 199.

[12] Hinton, *Biographical Portraiture*, 114.

[13] Hinton, *Biographical Portraiture*, 32–33.

renewed dedication of my soul to a covenant God in Christ. I trust it will be accepted with him. Amen.

September 4, 1798 [Tuesday][14]
Have thought this morning on David's prayer, "O forsake me not utterly."[15] It seems a suitable text: may I first feed on it myself, and then be directed of God to present its blessings to my people.

September 8, 1798 [Saturday][16]
I hope I have some assistance in study, but am rather low as to personal piety: O Lord, revive thy work![17] ... Have now, blessed be God, enjoyed some liberty in private prayer: O may it be attended with watchfulness, and followed by the expected blessing! May tomorrow be a sweet and profitable day.

September, 1798[18]
I am now setting off for Birmingham, under a conviction that it is my duty, though it is unpleasant to leave my family. O may the presence and protection of the most high God be with me, and give me success! My dear flock I commit to the care of the great Head of the church. But ah! where will they find, in this scarcity of ministers, a pastor, wise, faithful, judicious, and zealous: firm and yet candid; ardent and yet meek; neither despising nor relying on human learning: one who can unite various tempers, tastes and opinions; be respectable in the world, humble and simple in the church, and in all faithful to God. And yet their present pastor is deficient in all. God can send them one, every way better qualified to carry on his work. His holy will be done, and his name be glorified forever and ever! Amen.

---

14 Hinton, *Biographical Portraiture*, 114.
15 Psalm 119:8.
16 Hinton, *Biographical Portraiture*, 114.
17 Habakkuk 3:2.
18 Hinton, *Biographical Portraiture*, 159.

September, 1798 (1 week after departing for Birmingham)[19]
Arrived safely at home after a fatiguing, but, I thank God, a pleasant and prosperous journey; especially so to the temporal interests of my flock, for the Lord has given me favour in the eyes of the people, who have largely contributed to defray the expense attendant on our building.

October 4, 1798 [Thursday][20]
Not sufficiently alive to God; yet I hope careful not to offend him. Hope I have some better government of the passions.

October 5, 1798 [Friday][21]
Inclined to anger this morning: had a conflict, and hope I have overcome. Alas! I fear many things are not as they ought to be in my soul: but there is balm in Gilead, and a physician there.[22]

October 6, 1798 [Saturday][23]
Have been studying the proper method of governing the passions; O may divine grace aid me in the difficult work. On examination I find, 1. That the frame of my mind has not been very spiritual; 2. That the evils recorded on my birthday do many of them still exist in great power: yet I hope I have been more dead to human applause, more careful to guard against an angry temper, and more spiritual in conversation, for which I praise the God of my mercies. Still I am not alive in the closet as I ought to be, have not sufficient love for souls, do not improve my time, am grovelling in my affections, and too prone to anger: for these things I call my soul to deep humility and penitence, and apply afresh to the blood of sprinkling. This evening I give myself afresh to God and his service: my God, accept the surrender in my Saviour's name!

---

[19] Hinton, *Biographical Portraiture*, 159.
[20] Hinton, *Biographical Portraiture*, 33.
[21] Hinton, *Biographical Portraiture*, 33.
[22] Jeremiah 8:22.
[23] Hinton, *Biographical Portraiture*, 33.

October 7, 1798 [Sunday][24]
This has been a happy day: preached from, "He that hath no rule over his own spirit,"[25] &c. I hope it has been, and will be, a very useful sermon, and especially to my own unruly passions.

October 10, 1798 [Wednesday][26]
Today I found evil temper stirring again, and though not suffered to break out, yet a kind of commanding ill-humour (part gloominess of spirits, part moral depravity) troubled me: Lord, help me to overcome it through the blood of the Lamb, and to assume a happily cheerful and contented spirit—having so many things to be grateful for.

October 13, 1798 [Saturday][27]
This week has been chequered;[28] yet most cause to be grateful and encouraged. Hope devotion is on the increase, but still very deficient. Desire to be thankful for some liberty in secret devotion in prayer for my own soul, in my family, and among my flock: O may my great Intercessor present these poor prayers with acceptance to God, and may the Holy Spirit help me to watch for gracious answers!

October 19, 1798 [Friday][29]
Too apt to suffer the world to occupy my first morning thoughts, and to banish spirituality from all the day. May a gracious God forgive this fault, and help me to avoid it.

---

[24] Hinton, *Biographical Portraiture*, 114.

[25] Proverbs 25:28.

[26] Hinton, *Biographical Portraiture*, 33.

[27] Hinton, *Biographical Portraiture*, 34.

[28] *Chequered* meaning having both successful and unsuccessful periods of time.

[29] Hinton, *Biographical Portraiture*, 34.

October 20, 1798 [Saturday][30]
Happy in study, and expect a happy day tomorrow, because the Lord keeps me sensibly dependent on himself.

October 21, 1798 [Sunday][31]
Not disappointed: it has been a truly pleasant day, blessed be God.

October 22, 1798 [Monday][32]
Happy in the recollection of yesterday; the Sabbath has done me good: pleasant prayer meeting.

October 25, 1798 [Thursday][33]
Hope my soul is not entirely barren, but it is not as fruitful as I wish: Lord, revive thy work![34] Spent some time in reading Flavel's *Touchstone of Sincerity*.[35] My greatest danger of being deceived is in the following instances: 1. Lest under a profession of religion, the carnal mind should remain: 2. Lest I should be satisfied with having the passions occasionally impressed, without having habitually a sense of God's presence on my mind: 3. Lest I should delight in religion for its appendages, such as respect, present comfort, and deliverance from future misery, instead of possessing a hearty delight in the purity of God's nature, and the perfections of his delightful government: 4. Lest my constitutional sins be not truly embittered and subdued: 5. Lest I be better pleased with the religion that man observes, than that which God observes. In all there is danger: O may God make my evidences more clear.

---

[30] Hinton, *Biographical Portraiture*, 114.

[31] Hinton, *Biographical Portraiture*, 114.

[32] Hinton, *Biographical Portraiture*, 114.

[33] Hinton, *Biographical Portraiture*, 34.

[34] Habakkuk 3:2.

[35] John Flavel's (1630–1691) work *Touchstone of Sincerity; or, Trial of True and False Religion* was first published in 1679.

October 26, 1798. [Friday][36]
Visited—. Much pleased with the simplicity of her piety. I am grieved at her affliction, yet I rejoice that the High and Holy One who inhabiteth eternity, does evidently, according to his gracious promise, dwell in that poor cottage with "her that is of an humble and contrite spirit, and that trembleth at his word."[37] I make these remarks on my visit: That poor people are the more happy, because they have never been troubled with the unbelief that arises from converse with infidels or their writings: That the impress which religion makes on them is a great and striking evidence that it is of God: And that the happiness I have felt today is a proof that the work of Christ is its own reward. I think I hear him saying, "I was sick, and ye visited me"[38]

November 2, 1798 [Friday][39]
Much reason to complain of myself the past month, and especially in the last two weeks: a strange leanness and barrenness of soul, that is both afflicting and alarming; and I earnestly pray God to remove the influence of an evil heart of unbelief.

November 10, 1798 [Saturday][40]
Strange deadness. Oh what a conflict is human life! It is hard sometimes for me to think that mine is the conflict of a believer; yet, though I am faint, I desire to pursue—it is the only path of safety and of happiness. ... Some answers to prayer I desire thankfully to record, and to present renewed petitions that the poor preparation for tomorrow may be abundantly increased, by an enlargement of thought and a temper of heart, which the Holy Spirit alone can give.

---

[36] Hinton, *Biographical Portraiture*, 199.
[37] Isaiah 66:2.
[38] Matthew 25:36.
[39] Hinton, *Biographical Portraiture*, 34.
[40] Hinton, *Biographical Portraiture*, 34–35, 114.

December 1, 1798 [Saturday][41]

The past month has been a very mingled scene: the former part of it much injured by a kind of latent half infidelity, not arising to absolute unbelief, but so weakening faith as to leave me very faint; the last fortnight, blessed be God, I have been somewhat more at liberty. Have been enabled to redeem more time for the study, and hope I have some answers to prayer; but am still ashamed of my sluggishness. I do not seem to live as I ought. My revivals are of short duration. A great pressure of various concerns occupies too much of my thoughts and my time. Yet life is rapidly advancing, and tomorrow is the last Lord's supper day of another year: I hope I desire to be awakened to look well to my feet, to work the work of him that hath sent me while it is called today. I trust, I this evening, surrender myself afresh to the service of a covenant God in Christ, with all I have; and fall, a weak and helpless and guilty worm, on him who, I trust, will be made of God unto me wisdom and righteousness, and sanctification and redemption.[42]

December 2, 1798 [Sunday][43]

Morning was a very comfortable opportunity; afternoon not equally comfortable, but chiefly owing to bodily weakness: at the Lord's table I was much at liberty, and I trust truly and earnestly desirous of growing sanctification. On the whole it has been a very happy day; I have enjoyed life, and some liberty, in private as well as public. May the savour of this day long remain!

December 5, 1798 [Wednesday][44]

Have begun to feel my spiritual decline: O may the prayer of faith lay hold afresh on God!

---

[41] Hinton, *Biographical Portraiture*, 35.

[42] 1 Corinthians 1:30.

[43] Hinton, *Biographical Portraiture*, 114–115.

[44] Hinton, *Biographical Portraiture*, 35.

December 8. 1798 [Saturday][45]

Thank God, much time redeemed for study this week, and I hope a profitable week: yet I find, time without a heart for God is not sufficient. God give me more of both; and especially of a spirit of prayer, my great want.

December 17, 1798 [Monday][46]

If I do not live to return, let this be my last record: that I commit my soul into the hands of my covenant God in Christ, not unwilling to die, if that event be most for his glory; and not without a hope that my poor guilty and helpless soul has found an almighty and unchanging friend in the blessed Redeemer, who hath not, in the midst of all my backslidings, cast me off, and who will never utterly forsake me. I leave my dear partner, who has been to me a truly faithful, pious, and every way excellent companion, to the care of Almighty God, and with her the dear children, humbly hoping that he will be their Father, the guide of their youth, and their unfailing friend.

---

[45] Hinton, *Biographical Portraiture*, 35.

[46] Hinton, *Biographical Portraiture*, 91. Hinton had to make significant travel commitments to promote the grammar-school which he oversaw.

1799

January, 1799 [?][1]
Returned home safe, after an absence of nearly five weeks almost without intermission. Blessed be God who has kept my life in the midst of death, and given me uncommon success in my several visits, inclining the hearts of his people to be kind to me and to my flock.

January 26 [?], 1799 [Saturday][2]
My mind is very much dissipated, and unfit for study ... Obliged to take old sermons. God forgive the leanness and poverty of my soul!

February 2, 1799 [Saturday][3]
Thank God, very comfortable in study this morning: some liberty in prayer, and great hopes of his presence tomorrow.

April 7, 1799 [Sunday][4]
The morning was a very acceptable, I hope a useful, sermon. The hurry of the afternoon rather discomposed my spirits at the Lord's table: I was obliged to be short, in order to save time and strength for the evening; yet I hope it was a profitable day.

---

[1] Hinton, *Biographical Portraiture*, 160.
[2] Hinton, *Biographical Portraiture*, 160.
[3] Hinton, *Biographical Portraiture*, 115.
[4] Hinton, *Biographical Portraiture*, 115.

April 14, 1799 [Sunday][5]
The first part of Naaman's case; a very acceptable sermon, and I hope useful. Heard my brother West[6] in the afternoon, and enjoyed the sermon very much: preached in the evening.

April 23, 1799 [Tuesday][7]
I bless God that this year has been one of less anxiety to our minds than any one for several years past. My dear wife's health has been in a most comfortable state, and our family concerns have been conducted by a kind providence in a course of moderate prosperity. On rising this morning, I united with my dear wife in surrendering ourselves afresh to our covenant God, in committing to his kind providence and richer grace the children he hath given us, as well as the dear orphans; in imploring delivering goodness in an approaching trial; and in praying for grace to improve our abundant mercies to the glory of the Giver. O may "high Heaven," which heard, record these solemn vows, and assure to us an answer of peace!

June 12, 1799 [Wednesday][8]
Like too many days past, dull, heavy, forgetful of God, and harassed by a fretful and angry spirit; but, though cast down, I am not in despair, for Jesus lives, and therefore his people shall live also. There is a gracious promise, "sin shall not have dominion over you:"[9] Lord help me to believe it, and give me to experience its fulfilment for Christ's sake!

---

[5] Hinton, *Biographical Portraiture*, 115.

[6] Four of Hinton's siblings can be identified at this time: Thomas, West, and Hatton (sister), and John. On John see *Northampton Mercury*, Saturday 26 May 1787.

[7] Hinton, *Biographical Portraiture*, 73.

[8] Hinton, *Biographical Portraiture*, 35–36.

[9] Romans 6:14.

June 20, 1799 [Thursday][10]
Blessed be God, I have enjoyed a degree of life and pleasure in my work today, to which I have, alas, too long been a stranger. In both discourses, especially in the former, my heart was much enlarged, as also in the work of prayer, and in the solemn engagements of the Lord's table.

July 1, 1799 [Monday][11]
How fast do the months revolve! Each as it returns says, "Be not slothful:"[12] "*Dum vivimus vivamus.*"[13] Let me hear the voice, and not forget that it is more difficult to live Christ than to preach Christ: natural abilities have often sufficed for the latter, the former is the work of all-powerful grace. O Lord, engrave it on my heart to-day, that thou art with me!

Evening. This day has, I trust, been a day spent with God, and for God.

July 4 [?], 1799 [Thursday][14]
Not alive to God in the frame of my mind, though this is a very important day, and I hope I sincerely bless God for the deliverance of my dear wife, and the birth of my son Isaac;[15] yet I have not a heart to enjoy my mercies so spiritually as I wish. Natural spirits are low, and fatigue considerable.

July 10, 1799 [Wednesday][16]
I feel a strange darkness, a listlessness to divine things—which troubles me, but does not shake my hope in Christ: I trust I am seeking the cause, as far as it is moral, to implore its pardon; if it is natural, I am certain of the compassion of the Almighty.

---

[10] Hinton, *Biographical Portraiture*, 115.
[11] Hinton, *Biographical Portraiture*, 36.
[12] Romans 12:11; Hebrews 6:12.
[13] Latin translation: Let us live while we live.
[14] Hinton, *Biographical Portraiture*, 52.
[15] Isaac Hinton (1799–1847).
[16] Hinton, *Biographical Portraiture*, 36.

July 27, 1799 [Saturday][17]
Have reason to complain that my soul is not lively; I hardly know the cause—I pray to discover it. I have a cheerful hope of my acceptance in the Beloved, but not a lively sense of my privilege in being so. I hope I am on the foundation; but I wish to have the building grow up into Christ, its founder and its head.

September 25, 1799 [Wednesday][18]
Preached at Abingdon: not very comfortable—too much regard to men, and an over anxiety to do well; yet on the whole, I believe my views good, and I thank God for his assistance.

September 27, 1799 [Friday][19]
On examining the past month, I hope I have somewhat grown in grace; but alas! very slowly. The former part of the month was dull and unfruitful. I still find myself too prone to earthly enjoyments, too little alive in the frame of my mind, too apt to speak hasty words, and above all harassed with a latent infidelity, an evil heart of unbelief. Yet on the whole I make a record of gratitude: an Ebenezer I again raise, though with mingled joy and sorrow, mourning and gratitude. Some seasons of private prayer (the best test of sincerity) have, I trust, been solemn and sincere, and indulged with the divine presence.

October 20, 1799 [Sunday][20]
Rather dull in the morning; crowded with worldly thoughts: grew better as the day advanced.

---

[17] Hinton, *Biographical Portraiture*, 36.
[18] Hinton, *Biographical Portraiture*, 115.
[19] Hinton, *Biographical Portraiture*, 36–37.
[20] Hinton, *Biographical Portraiture*, 115.

October 22, 1799 [Tuesday][21]
"The slothful man roasteth not that which he took in hunting."[22] Such in spiritual things am I: I pray and strive earnestly for comfort, and then carelessly let it go again, as though it were not worth the keeping.

November 10, 1799 [Sunday][23]
Comfortable afternoon: In the evening the Sunday-school sermon, and very comfortable for such a service, but wish it were more spiritual: yet thank God for a large congregation, and a very good collection. Comfort should not be all my care; usefulness should be studied, and be itself my comfort.

November 16, 1799 [Saturday][24]
Overdone with constant cares—and a sad depravity of heart, not improving what strength I have: I never had more reason for humility and penitence, nor more need of mercy and grace to help. I hope on the whole my heart is right with God, and the tendency of my constant and best affections towards heaven; but my soul is not in health, it does not prosper as I could wish. "Save now, O Lord! O Lord, I beseech thee send now prosperity!"[25]

---

[21] Hinton, *Biographical Portraiture*, 37
[22] Proverbs 12:27.
[23] Hinton, *Biographical Portraiture*, 115.
[24] Hinton, *Biographical Portraiture*, 37.
[25] Psalm 118:25.

1800

February 9, 1800 [Sunday][1]

Preached only in the afternoon. "It is the Lord, let him do what seemeth him good,"[2] a funeral sermon for Mr.—'s child. A pleasant season; the subject applied well to my own indisposition, and is, I hope, the sentiment of my heart.

February 18, 1800 [Tuesday][3]

This evening there was a meeting of friends at the vestry, who subscribed liberally to procure an assistant preacher: blessed be God. I trust it is in answer to many prayers that he would send me aid in my ministerial work, and afford me heart and time for private communion with himself.

February 23, 1800 [Sunday][4]

A second Sabbath I am prevented from speaking in the name of the Lord, or nearly so, having only addressed my dear people a few moments at the end of a sermon delivered by Mr. Raban:[5] yet I have

---

[1] Hinton, *Biographical Portraiture*, 116.

[2] 1 Samuel 3:18.

[3] Hinton, *Biographical Portraiture*, 163.

[4] Hinton, *Biographical Portraiture*, 163.

[5] Thomas Raban (1734–1802) was a minister to the Independent Congregation at Yardley. He was ordained on June 12, 1783. See Letter from William Cowper to John Newton, June 17, 1783 in Thomas Wright, *Correspondence of William Cowper* (New York: Dodd, Mead, and Company/London: Hodder and Stoughton, n.d), II, 80; Thomas Coleman, *Memoirs of the Independent Churches in Northamptonshire* (London: John Snow, 1853, 292–295); "Memoir of the Life of the Reverend Thomas Raban," in *The Evangelical Magazine and Missionary Chronicle* 11 (January 1803): 3–7.

cheerful hope that this suspension of my labours will be but temporary, and that I shall not die, but live, and declare the works of the Lord. My mind is dull in a considerable degree: it has calmness and resignation, but it much needs life and activity.

March 2, 1800 [Sunday][6]
Favoured to day with liberty to preach once more to my beloved flock, and was much affected in addressing them from Titus i. 1–3. I pray God it may not be without effect. I have ardently desired, and hoped, that it may prove the conversion of some soul. I thank God I have been very comfortable, both in private and public.

March 7, 1800 [Friday][7]
Not so happy today, but the fault is my own: I have not been diligent, nor self-denying, nor watchful in my temper and conduct.

March 9, 1800 [Sunday][8]
At the Lord's table very comfortable: O may it be more lasting than on the last ordinance day! ... Great Shepherd and Bishop of souls, take me under thy care! Lead me and guide me for thy name's sake, O Lord! I trust in thee to fulfil the promise, "He shall subdue our iniquities."[9]

March 10, 1800 [Monday][10]
I desire to record with gratitude that I have not pleaded the above promise in vain. Though I have not preserved a perfect equanimity this day (and I desire to be humble for my sin on this account) yet I have received answers to prayer, and bless God that my

---

[6] Hinton, *Biographical Portraiture*, 163–164.

[7] Hinton, *Biographical Portraiture*, 37.

[8] Hinton, *Biographical Portraiture*, 37, 116. The biographer has omitted "O may it be more lasting than on the last ordinance day!" from the March 9, 1800 entry on page 37.

[9] Micah 7:19.

[10] Hinton, *Biographical Portraiture*, 37.

constitutional sin has not reigned. O may grace reign more and more in me, unto life eternal!

March 12, 1800 [Wednesday][11]
My mind seems in a great measure lifeless as to divine things: I desire to search out the cause, and hope to have it removed at a throne of grace.

March 13, 1800 [Thursday][12]
Still mourning a cold and carnal heart; still longing for a more spiritual frame, and hoping that I observe some signs of dawning day.

March 14, 1800 [Friday][13]
I hope this has been a day of some carefulness in my conduct; and certainly of too much of that carefulness of which the apostle says, "I would have you without"[14] it. I am also much injured by secret suggestions of unbelief: I have not the confidence in gospel promises I ought to have, considering how often they have been fulfilled to others, and to myself. I mourn also a want of spirituality in my affections: my soul cleaveth unto the dust, and the enemy is very busy in endeavouring to keep me from thee; but "quicken thou me according to thy word!"[15]

March 17, 1800 [Monday][16]
Have to observe in my mind a sinful anxiety to preach well, rather than a holy anxiety to preach usefully: I fear I rather seek my own honour than God's. I confess this sin; I trust. I repent of it from my heart. I hope for its forgiveness, and its removal from my breast. Oh

---

[11] Hinton, *Biographical Portraiture*, 37.
[12] Hinton, *Biographical Portraiture*, 38.
[13] Hinton, *Biographical Portraiture*, 38.
[14] 1 Corinthians 7:32.
[15] Psalm 119:25.
[16] Hinton, *Biographical Portraiture*, 116.

how deceitful is this heart of mine, and what a gracious God to hold any communication with me.

For pride, that busy sin,
  Spoils all that I perform:
Cursed pride, that unawares creeps in,
  And swells a feeble worm.

March 18, 1800 [Tuesday][17]
Having confessed this sin, I hope I have obtained pardon and the renewed help of God, for he giveth grace to the humble. "He speaketh peace to his people; but let them not turn again to folly."[18]

March 22, 1800 [Saturday][19]
This has been a happy day. The week has been much chequered by many secret suggestions of unbelief from a cruel foe. O God, do thou bruise Satan under the feet of thy unworthy servant.[20] I trust I am thine; O save me!

March 27, 1800 [Thursday][21]
Still considerably dark and cold in my mind; but greatly refreshed in secret devotion in the evening, and helped to wrestle with God for myself, my family, and my flock, and the success of the Redeemer's cause. The Lord will, I trust, fulfill these petitions, for the sake of my great High Priest and Intercessor on high.

March 29, 1800 [Saturday][22]
Engaged in rather unprofitable conversation with a young minister; too much on nice, rather than on profitable points. I beg forgiveness

---

[17] Hinton, *Biographical Portraiture*, 116.
[18] Psalm 85:8.
[19] Hinton, *Biographical Portraiture*, 38.
[20] Romans 16:10.
[21] Hinton, *Biographical Portraiture*, 38.
[22] Hinton, *Biographical Portraiture*, 292.

of God, and hope for strength for future days. At the same time, I pray God that the conversation of the day may not have an unfriendly influence on the work of the Sabbath that is approaching. May its evils be removed by communion with God in secret, a lively spirit of devotion, a strong regard to the interest of immortal souls, and an ardent desire to promote the interest of the Redeemer's kingdom!

April 1, 1800 [Tuesday][23]

On reviewing the past month I find it full of vicissitude;[24] much reason for gratitude, much for humility and pious sorrow. I hope sin hath not reigned, and I have had some lively and spiritual days; O that every day might be a day of communion with God! I fly to the blood of sprinkling for pardon, and I hope for the sealing influences of the blessed Spirit on the coming day, and especially at the Lord's table. Life must be chequered; but O that the spiritual life had fewer dark days! Lift thou up, O Lord, the light of thy countenance upon me![25] I am on the whole much encouraged.

April 17 [Thursday], 19 [Saturday], 1800[26]

Considerably harassed by the enemy of souls leading to doubt the foundations of religion: O may the darkened cloud withdraw! I humbly hope I am willing to be tried, so that I may but come forth as gold.[27] Lord, strengthen thou my faith! Blessed Redeemer, thou hast prayed that it may not fail.[28]

---

[23] Hinton, *Biographical Portraiture*, 38–39.

[24] *Vicissitude* meaning a change of circumstance, typically negative and unwelcome.

[25] Psalm 4:6.

[26] Hinton, *Biographical Portraiture*, 39.

[27] Job 23:10.

[28] Luke 22:32.

April 27, 1800 [Sunday][29]

Baptized eleven persons at Abingdon, among whom is my dear wife, hitherto a paedobaptist. Her attendance on this ordinance, I rejoice to say, is a voluntary tribute to the dictates of conscience and the honour of Christ; and in this view I think highly indeed of her conduct. She had no motive of a domestic kind, for the affection of her husband was entirely hers; and his approbation too, so long as she saw not the command of Christ full and clear to direct her personal obedience. I bless God that not the least disaffection—I think I may add, not the possibility of it—existed on account of this difference of opinion: and I am particularly thankful, that I have never spoken one word that could induce her to think I should be more happy if she were a baptist. The Lord has been her only teacher, and the throne of grace her only place of converse on this subject: but her cheerful willingness to follow the blessed Redeemer, and to do whatsoever he has commanded, has certainly given an additional evidence of uprightness of heart, and a desire to glorify him who gave himself for her. May the blessing of our covenant God rest on this transaction, and render it an additional cement to our affection and a blessing to our children!

May 3, 1800 [Saturday][30]

Still attacked by the enemy with his fiery darts, and subject to an awful darkness of mind which, though it does not destroy my hope, prevents the comfort of it. I have found some relief in prayer, and some hope in reflecting that the adorable Redeemer once said, "My God, my God, why hast thou forsaken me?"[31] I indeed suffer justly, but my blessed Lord had done nothing amiss: let me then patiently wait for the salvation of my God.[32]

---

[29] Hinton, *Biographical Portraiture*, 74.

[30] Hinton, *Biographical Portraiture*, 39.

[31] Psalm 22:1; Matthew 27:46.

[32] Lamentations 3:25–26.

May 25, 1800 [Sunday][33]
A very good day: but the evening spoiled with wretched pride and self-complacency; a mischievous weed, deep rooted, which all my winter seasons have not yet killed. O may it be at length rooted out!

July 4, 1800 [Friday][34]
Thanks to our great Preserver, I returned home and found all safe. The health of my body is benefited, the health of my soul (I fear) somewhat injured: for such are my weakness and negligence, that I do not seem to have walked closely with God during the journey. O what an ungrateful and treacherous heart!

July 6, 1800 Sunday Evening[35]
I have been looking back in this diary: Oh, what chequered scenes does it present to my view! But, great God, what shall be its close? Its termination will soon come; alas! that my evidences should still be so dull! I seem to make no progress in the way to heaven, no advance of character: and this grieves my soul, which is weak and discouraged by the attacks of unbelief. Still my whole reliance is on the gospel; I not only believe it to be true, but venture my everlasting all upon its promises. But O that my faith were more strong! Yet if it be best, I hope I am willing to be thus tried, that my faith, though it be tried with fire, may be found unto praise and honour and glory, at the appearing of the great God and my Saviour, Jesus Christ.[36] To him, to him be glory forever! Amen.[37]

July 14, 1800 [Monday][38]
Lively in frame, but fear much of self creeps in: God accept and forgive me through Christ! Spent the evening at home in converse with

[33] Hinton, *Biographical Portraiture*, 116.
[34] Hinton, *Biographical Portraiture*, 91.
[35] Hinton, *Biographical Portraiture*, 39.
[36] 1 Peter 1:8.
[37] Romans 11:36.
[38] Hinton, *Biographical Portraiture*, 116–117.

my family, and other acts of domestic devotion. A day for much thanksgiving; may its effect be growing sanctification and nearness to God.

August 23, 1800 [Saturday][39]
I trust some revival in my soul this day; yet considerable darkness and unbelief.

> Oh! what a wretched land is this,
> That yields me no supply:[40]

but how gracious is he who maketh springs to flow in the desert.

September 3, 1800 [Wednesday][41]
On reviewing the past year, I hardly know which disposition should most prevail—sorrow for my wretched returns to divine mercy, or gratitude for the continuance of so many undeserved and abused favours. Oh my wretched, wretched heart of unbelief! here, here the mischief lies.

> And shall I ever live
> At this poor dying rate?[42]

Yet hope springs up. Blessed Jesus! on thee I cast my weary soul; still I hope, still I trust in thee. Shall I live to see September 3, 1801? O sovereign Disposer of all things, thou alone knowest: but if thou so determine, O grant, for the sake of my adorable Redeemer, for the happiness of thy people, and the glory of thy name, that fewer dark, gloomy, worldly days, may be found in this year. O God! help,

---

[39] Hinton, *Biographical Portraiture*, 40.

[40] Isaac Watts, "Our journey is a thorny maze," stanza 1.

[41] Hinton, *Biographical Portraiture*, 40.

[42] Isaac Watts, "Breathing after the Holy Spirit; or, Fervency of devotion desired," stanza 4.

help me from thy throne! Save thy servant that putteth his trust in thee![43]

September 4, 1800 [Thursday][44]

Alas! still dull and heavy; perhaps chiefly through weariness, fatigue, and ill health, little able to withstand the temptations of the enemy, and the risings of corruption.

October 3, 1800 [Friday][45]

I desire to be humbled that this has been a dull unfruitful month. I have been very poorly and low in my spirits, of which the enemy takes advantage.

October 4, 1800 [Saturday][46]

Somewhat revived, and desirous to search and try my ways, and turn again unto the Lord. What have been the causes of my unfruitfulness during the past month 1. Corrupt nature, indwelling sin. 2. Want of watchfulness against it. 3. The secret temptations of Satan to unbelief. 4. Neglect of secret prayer, both stated and ejaculatory. 5. Pride and self-complacency attending, and especially following, comfort in duty. Oh, what a host of foes within and without, but chiefly within! How necessary to humble myself before God, and to gird on afresh the armour of the gospel, that I may stand in the evil day, and having done all may stand.[47] Blessed be God, there is yet hope. "It is of his mercy that I am not consumed, and because his tender compassions fail not: this I call to mind, therefore have I hope."[48] Here, Lord, I consecrate myself to thee afresh; receive the surrender, and ratify it in heaven that my Beloved is mine and I am his forever.[49]

---

[43] Psalm 86:2.

[44] Hinton, *Biographical Portraiture*, 40.

[45] Hinton, *Biographical Portraiture*, 40.

[46] Hinton, *Biographical Portraiture*, 40–41.

[47] Ephesians 6:13.

[48] Lamentations 3:22.

[49] Song of Songs 2:16.

October 8, 1800 [Wednesday][50]
Still my spiritual enemies are strong and lively, and the perverseness of the youth in school is a severe trial to my patience, which, alas, is very weak. I have not attained to the happy art of uniting activity and fortitude, with gentleness and sweetness of temper; yet I follow after that I may attain: may God help me.

October 28 [Tuesday], 30 [Thursday], 1800[51]
Too eager in the midst of worldly cares, but decidedly proposing the glory of my divine Master.

November 16, 1800 [Sunday][52]
Confined by pain in my head and face: preached only in the evening for the Sunday-school. A large congregation—respectable in the eyes of the world: God grant this may not be all! How apt is human favour to puff up a vain and empty mind: may God forgive and subdue this disposition!

Not dated, 1800[53]
I thank God, we found the state of the church matter for praise.

---

[50] Hinton, *Biographical Portraiture*, 90.

[51] Hinton, *Biographical Portraiture*, 41.

[52] Hinton, *Biographical Portraiture*, 117.

[53] This entry occurs after "an evening spent with the deacons." According to Hinton's biographer, "Frequent mention occurs, also, of conversations held with candidates and inquirers; and on one occasion he says, 'May God send me many such visitors. It is pleasant and, I hope, useful employ.'" Hinton, *Biographical Portraiture*, 163.

1801

January 1, 1801 [Thursday][1]
This morning rose early; was particular, and I hope earnest in prayer to God. I have reason to look back on the past year with most lively gratitude to God, my great preserver and benefactor. In spiritual concerns, I find that most of my Sabbaths have been comfortable ones, though many have been dull. More of darkness and unbelief than has been usual for some years past; yet I think these trials have been productive of good: I think they have induced greater degrees of self-abasement, and of spirituality of mind. "Bless the Lord, O my soul, and all that is within me, bless his holy name."[2]

March 31, 1801 [Tuesday][3]
A happy month, though attended oft with languor of spirit, and want of ardour in devotion, as well as too great anxiety on account of the pressure of the times. More sensible than ever, I hope, of the evil of a fretful spirit; I trust not more indulgent towards it, but the contrary.

April 2, 1801 [Thursday][4]
This has been a very solemn and impressive day, both in preaching and at the Lord's table: O may its influence be abundant and abiding!

---

[1] Hinton, *Biographical Portraiture*, 41.
[2] Psalm 103:1.
[3] Hinton, *Biographical Portraiture*, 41–42.
[4] Hinton, *Biographical Portraiture*, 117.

April 23, 1801 [Thursday][5]
This is the anniversary of my marriage to a pious, prudent, and truly excellent companion; concerning whom, I bless God, I have no doubt but she is an heir, and I hope I am a fellow-heir, of the grace of life.[6] The past year seems to have been one of increasing happiness and spirituality, and comfort of every kind to us.

September 3, 1801 [Thursday][7]
Forty years long, O Lord, hast thou led me in the wilderness, and surely I have too much of that unbelieving and perverse spirit with which thou wast grieved in the children of Israel. The past year does not afford that regular improvement I could wish. I hope my character is improved; but, alas, how little is the fruit I bring forth unto God. How great the mercy that still spares an unfruitful plant! My great complaint still is unbelief, irregular piety, backwardness to come to the throne of grace, and inability to appear in the school, in the parlour, and in conversation, what I am in the pulpit: O Lord, help me! that I may by a pious and spiritual conversation, more eminently adorn the doctrine of God my Saviour.[8] I hope I do with much solemnity and sincerity again consecrate myself to thee.

September 6, 1801 [Sunday][9]
I thank my God that this has been a pleasant day, and especially at the Lord's table: O may the savour of it long remain! I hope I could say at the close of it, "Mine eyes have seen thy salvation."[10]

---

[5] Hinton, *Biographical Portraiture*, 51.
[6] 1 Peter 3:7.
[7] Hinton, *Biographical Portraiture*, 42.
[8] Titus 2:10.
[9] Hinton, *Biographical Portraiture*, 117.
[10] Luke 2:30.

September 7, 1801 [Monday][11]
Spent in some good degree, I hope, under the influence of the truth contemplated on the past Sabbath. Blessed be God for ordinances, and more for his Spirit in them.

September 10, 1801 [Thursday][12]
Rather too anxious in considering a subject for a missionary sermon. O that I had more faith!

September 12, 1801 [Saturday][13]
Very comfortable in the study in the evening; hope I have received help of God. "Not unto me, not unto me, but unto thy name be the glory."[14]

---

[11] Hinton, *Biographical Portraiture*, 117.
[12] Hinton, *Biographical Portraiture*, 117.
[13] Hinton, *Biographical Portraiture*, 117.
[14] Psalm 115:1.

1802

January 11, 1802 [Monday][1]
Yesterday was a very cold uncomfortable opportunity at the table of the Lord: I fear that he withholds his presence.

March 6, 1802 [Saturday] Review of the Month[2]
Some very comfortable seasons in the closet. Not so great reason as at sometimes to lament the prevalence of indwelling corruption: blessed be he that teacheth my hands to war and my fingers to fight.[3] I overcome through the blood of the Lamb.[4] But much cause to lament frequent backwardness to closet exercises, and coldness in them. If a saint, I am one of very low attainments; I hope it is a matter of deep humility.

March 15, 1802 [Monday][5]
The evening spent in prayer on the particular case of a youth distressed by conviction and despondency.

June [?], 1802[6]
May God send to my dear flock a pastor after his own heart! I entreat them to follow that spirit of meekness, forbearance, and constant regard to the Redeemer's interest in preference to their own views, of which I have for fifteen years past endeavoured to set them an example. I trust to meet them, very many of them, as my joy and crown in the day of the Lord Jesus.

---

[1] Hinton, *Biographical Portraiture*, 117.
[2] Hinton, *Biographical Portraiture*, 42.
[3] Psalm 144:1.
[4] Revelation 12:11.
[5] Hintion, *Biographical Portraiture*, 203.
[6] Hinton, *Biographical Portraiture*, 164.

June 16, 1802 [Wednesday][7]
Comfortable in some religious exercises, but the impression soon wears away; yet I trust I do not presume in still cleaving to the great confidence of my soul, Christ Jesus, the same yesterday, today and forever.[8]

August 6, 1802 [Friday][9]
My mind is studious, and I hope devout: but the exertions of yesterday have lowered too much the tone of its active powers. What a mercy, that the consolations of religion are founded on a basis far more stable than that of frames and feelings; on Jesus, "the same yesterday, today, and forever."[10] I thank God, however, that I feel very cautious today, lest my head or heart, or hands, should offend against him.

September [?], 1802[11]
This week I have received a pressing invitation from the Rev. Mr. Fawcett[12] of Hebden Bridge, in Yorkshire, to undertake the care of an infant seminary for the purpose of training young men to the ministry. I cannot bear to think of leaving my people; yet if the will of God were that I should, I hope I should submit. But at present it does not appear to be my duty. Nothing could be a greater affliction to me than my removal; except it were the decline of the interest under my care—that would be much greater: but I pray God to prevent both ... I have requested a meeting of my friends, the deacons of the church here, to consult what answer I should return; and as I desire to have no will of my own, but to ask of God, with simplicity and godly sincerity, to give me wisdom, I trust I shall obtain it.

---

[7] Hinton, *Biographical Portraiture*, 42.

[8] Hebrews 13:8.

[9] Hinton, *Biographical Portraiture*, 117–118.

[10] Hebrews 13:8.

[11] Hinton, *Biographical Portraiture*, 166–167.

[12] John Fawcett (1739–1817) was a hymn writer, and pastor of Wainsgate Baptist Church in Hebden Bridge, West Yorkshire, England. He is the author of the famous hymn, "Blest Be the Tie that Binds."

September 3, 1802 [Friday][13]

Another year of my short life is past, and still a chequered scene lies in the retrospect, a mixture of good and evil, both natural and moral: in the former instance, good certainly prevails; in the latter it is, I fear, but doubtful. Pardon for the past and strength for the future, O Lord, is my desire. I hope I grow in grace. It is my preponderating opinion in the sight of God, that my character, blessed be his name, is improving: but ah! what sad imperfection still remains.

> Awake my soul, stretch every nerve,
> And press with vigour on:
> A heavenly race demands thy zeal,
> And an immortal crown.[14]

... The Lord's table not quite so comfortable: sad to say, checked by the presence of a brother from giving free utterance to my heart.

October 9, 1802 [Saturday][15]

A day in which I have discovered in a very large degree my own insufficiency for the arduous work of the ministry: I hope I am humbled, and I need humbling more. I am led to a throne of grace, and I trust my cries in some measure have been heard: O may my soul still wait on the Lord!

October 21, 1802 [Thursday][16]

The last four days have not been remarkable for elevation or depression; rather inclining to dulness, but not without refreshment of spirit, and a general conscious regard to the will of God, as under his eye: yet I lament that I have not more life and vigour in divine things. I carry about a body with a strong propensity to sin, and tending both

---

[13] Hinton, *Biographical Portraiture*, 42–43, 118.

[14] Philip Doddridge (1702–1751), "Awake, my soul, stretch every nerve," stanza 1.

[15] Hinton, *Biographical Portraiture*, 118.

[16] Hinton, *Biographical Portraiture*, 43.

to natural and spiritual death; but I trust in the gracious Redeemer that I shall at length, having sustained the conflict, obtain also the victory.

November 13, 1802 [Saturday][17]

I desire to be effectually humbled for my great barrenness, when retiring to study for my public work. I trust it has checked (what one day shall be killed, and I long for the death of it) the vanity and love of applause which dwell, but I bless God do not reign, within my heart.

December 19, 1802 [Sunday][18]

I am about to go to London tomorrow, with eight or nine pupils. Have experienced a very pleasant evening in taking a review of the past year, and an affectionate leave of my dear family; we have mutually commended ourselves to God in that delightful hymn of Dr. Doddridge, which closes—

> And if that joy no more be known,
> Give us to meet around thy throne![19]

The Lord hear our prayers, and fulfil the petitions of his servants. "Blessed be God, even the God of our salvation, who daily loadeth us with benefits."[20] It is fit a year of mercies should be closed with these thankful songs. Blessed fountain, that cleanses from all iniquity. Blessed Mediator and Intercessor, who encourages our hearts! To the triune God be immortal praise. Amen.

---

[17] Hinton, *Biographical Portraiture*, 118.
[18] Hinton, *Biographical Portraiture*, 91–92.
[19] Philip Doddridge, "The Christian Farewell," stanza 4.
[20] Psalm 69:19.

Autumn 1802[21]
My eldest son[22] is afflicted, and I fear the commencement of a consumption: my feelings have been much interested, and "all the father rises in my heart." I bless God, my chief desire is for his dear, his immortal soul: O God, do thou incline him to give it into the Saviour's hands, and then I can cheerfully resign him to thy will. I ought to bear cheerfully the share of affliction which thy infinite wisdom and goodness appoint: but, O! if it be consistent with thy will, if it be possible, let the bitter cup pass! Let the dear child live in this world; or if not, O let the prayers and tears of his parents, and above all the intercession of the dear Redeemer, prevail on his behalf, that his soul may live in thy sight! Let me be quickened to a more faithful discharge of my parental duties to him and to all my dear children; then welcome that affliction which brings us nearer to thee! Earthly physicians are very kind, but thou only canst bid the child live, either naturally or spiritually, and to thee, O God, I resign him: pardon my neglect, quicken my attention, and work in me the work of faith with power.

---

[21] Hinton, *Biographical Portraiture*, 76–77.

[22] John Howard Hinton (1791–1873). The author of *Biographical Portraiture*. He was 12 years old in this entry, and the illness lasted several years before his health improved (Hinton, *Biographical Portraiture*, 77).

1803

January 2, 1803 [Sunday][1]
A most truly happy day, blessed be God. I the more desire to praise him, because yesterday, through the absolute necessity of providing sermons for the Sabbath, I had not my usual opportunity for secret and solemn devotion: and I fear I have not sufficient care and fortitude to redeem time for that purpose.

January 13, 1803 [Thursday][2]
God willing, I set off tomorrow for London: O may my journey be accompanied with his blessing! The Lord preserve me from all evil: the Lord preserve my soul! To him I leave my dear partner and children, not knowing what a day may bring forth; but fully believing that my Redeemer is the "same yesterday, today, and forever."[3] My mind is calm and comfortable.

After prayer. Blessed be God for some holy freedom and humble confidence in prayer. It is good for me to draw near to God. I now leave my dear family with pleasure, believing that the Lord will be their God, that he will give grace and glory, and withhold no good thing from them that walk uprightly. "O Lord God of hosts, blessed is the man that trusteth in thee."[4]

March 13, 1803 [Sunday][5]
Lately, more dull and heavy days than I recollect for some years past; doubtless there are due reasons for it, though I cannot with precision specify them. Of the duties such a frame demands, I am

---

1 Hinton, *Biographical Portraiture*, 118.
2 Hinton, *Biographical Portraiture*, 92.
3 Hebrews 13:8.
4 Revelation 22:5.
5 Hinton, *Biographical Portraiture*, 43.

more certain I ought to examine: to humble myself before God, to search out the idols of my heart, and turn again unto the Lord with weeping and supplication.

April 2, 1803 [Saturday][6]
My life, always crowded with cares, has for some weeks past been over-crowded: yet I dare not excuse myself wholly, that I have not taken the active pleasure and delight in the ways of God which I desire and ought to feel. My Sabbaths have been pleasant, and some seasons of private devotion, but there is a considerable degree of dulness in my habitual frame: for this I hope I have been deeply humbled, and desire still to be so, before God. Within these two weeks past, I think I see and feel the rising of the blessed Sun of righteousness, with healing in his wings.

> Come, dearest Lord, descend and dwell
> By faith and love within my breast.[7]

August 3, 1803 [Wednesday][8]
Often unable to find subjects for the pulpit; and distressed on this account. Dull—looking to cisterns rather than the fountain; yet hitherto the Lord hath helped me. This evening is pleasant, and pleasant my work; pleasant too, I hope, will be the day of God: grant it, O Lord, for thy mercy's sake! Let tomorrow be the beginning of months unto me and mine; for the Redeemer's sake, Amen.

---

[6] Hinton, *Biographical Portraiture*, 43–44.
[7] Isaac Watts, "Come dearest Lord," stanza 1.
[8] Hinton, *Biographical Portraiture*, 118.

1804

January 1, 1804 [Sunday][1]
This has been a happy commencement of the new year; but my spirit is bowed down with the fear that neither my own soul nor the souls of my people are as lively as they have been wont to be.

January 11, 1804 [Wednesday][2]
I am leaving home again for a fortnight. O what a crowded world! How full of cares! Lord, I cast them all on thee. O that I could think more of my heavenly inheritance: yet I hope, through rich grace, I do not lose sight of it. Lord I commit to thee my family. If I return not, be thou the husband of the widow, and father of the fatherless! Let these lines stand as an assurance of the unaltered and hearty attachment of a husband and a father. If I return, O let it be with a blessing! For this I wish to live, that I may receive more from thee, do more for thee, be more happy in thee, and grow daily more like thee, O my God! ... Amiable partner! if thou survivest me, let the pledges of our love never forget they had a father who wished, above all things, that they might far exceed his piety and usefulness on earth, and then be reunited to him in heaven. Dear children regard, next to the counsels of God, those of the best of mothers.

April 23, 1804 [Monday][3]
Fourteen years ago this day, I led to the altar my beloved Ann: blessed be God, whose direction I then sought, and whose blessing I have ever since experienced. Our affection is sanctified and confirmed by religious principle: it increases with advancing life, and is

---

[1] Hinton, *Biographical Portraiture*, 118–119.
[2] Hinton, *Biographical Portraiture*, 92–93.
[3] Hinton, *Biographical Portraiture*, 51.

the source of daily and innumerable benefits to ourselves and our family. Blessed, forever blessed, be the name of our great benefactor and preserver! Amen!

September [?], 1804[4]

Much discouraged ... I sometimes fear that my usefulness in this city declines.

September 8, 1804 [Saturday][5]

For a considerable time past this diary has been neglected; I fear, not without incurring some guilt. I have been exceedingly thronged with business, and distressed for a time beyond all former example; my health also has been such that the weariness of the evening has left me hardly time or strength for devotion, and my mind oftentimes so discouraged that I had no spirit to write: yet I cannot excuse myself that something has not been done. Of late, blessed be God, my health and spirits have become more vigorous, and I hope in his strength to renew this soul-profiting exercise.

---

[4] Hinton, *Biographical Portraiture*, 172.
[5] Hinton, *Biographical Portraiture*, 45.

1805

January 1, 1805 [Tuesday][1]
Began the day with solemn prayer. Met my dear people in the evening; was solemn and spiritual, and set out afresh for the happy land, in divine strength. Spoke comfortably from the words, "I will be with thee."[2]

April 23, 1805 [Tuesday][3]
My diary of late has been sadly neglected, and I think of this circumstance with deep regret; yet such has been my weakness and ill state of health, that I have often thought it my duty not to attempt even the least addition to my absolutely necessary work...

Review of mercies. The great aid and comfort which I had in visiting a poor convict,[4] who was executed March 25, at our county prison, with such strong evidences of conversion and salvation, that I am bound to thank God on his behalf, and on my own also, that I was made to him a minister of mercy.

August 17, 1805 [Saturday][5]
It has been a comfortable week, only harassed occasionally by unbelieving thoughts, and a sceptical disposition—rather, however, subtracting from the influence of faith, than directly opposing it.

---

[1] Hinton, *Biographical Portraiture*, 119.

[2] Exodus 3:12; cf. Isaiah 43:2.

[3] Hinton, *Biographical Portraiture*, 45, 248.

[4] See James Hinton, *Narrative of the behavior and death of Thomas Davis* (London, 1805); Hinton, *Biographical Portraiture*, 236–246.

[5] Hinton, *Biographical Portraiture*, 44.

1806

September [2–5?], 1806[1]

This has been a solemn week. On Monday died my dear friend and brother Mr. Thomas Pasco,[2] aged only fifty-three, after a very short but triumphant illness. I have felt much, and have almost sunk beneath the depression of spirits which this event, and its attendant duties, have occasioned: I hope and pray that the succeeding advantages to my spiritual interests, and to those of my dear people, may be great indeed. His death was most triumphantly animating.

---

[1] Hinton, *Biographical Portraiture*, 170.

[2] Thomas Pasco (1753/54–1806) served as deacon for twenty-six years at the Baptist congregation in Oxford. He was a deacon when Hinton was called to minister, and proved to be a cherished friend. In a letter to the Baptist Association, Hinton writes of Pasco's death: "The greatest loss which the interest of Christ among us has sustained, is that of an highly esteemed brother who had been for twenty-six years a deacon of this church, and had zealously laboured for its peace and prosperity. In the midst of growing usefulness, and surrounded by the prayers and tears of the whole society, he was called to his eternal rest. His dying advice, his generous care to promote the gospel, and the high consolations of his departing hour, we hope to remember to our spiritual and everlasting profit." Hinton, *Biographical Portraiture*, 170, cf. 109, 110, 165, 253, 281; Pasco was also a Druggist/Chemist of Oxford, Oxfordshire. See "Memoir of the Late Mr. Thomas Pasco," *The Evangelical Magazine and Missionary Chronicle* 14 (November 1806): 481–487. He died on Monday September 1, and was buried on September 5, 1806 in Abingdon, Berkshire. I am indebted to Ron Heyboer for helping find this information in "Thomas Pasco," England and Wales Non-Conformist Record Indexes (RG4-8), 1588–1944.

September 6, 1806 [Saturday][3]
My health and spirits have been lately very low. I hope I have not sinned by neglecting my diary; God knoweth my frame: if I endeavour to gain more time, my strength sinks under the attempt.

[3] Hinton, *Biographical Portraiture*, 45.

1807

Day Unknown, 1807[1]
My mind is low as to my spiritual concerns. I am much worn down with constant fatigue in the school, visiting the sick and dying, &c. beyond my strength, which accounts for my lowness in some degree; and the enemy always attacks the weak, and often in a storm.

[1] Hinton, *Biographical Portraiture*, 175.

1810

May 5, 1810 [Saturday][1]
On examination I think fear prevails. I have of late been very dull.

> How low my hope of joys above,
> How few affections there.[2]

Much discouraged by reflecting on the hardness, coldness, and unbelief of my own heart. My views of its dreadful sinfulness, have of late been almost overwhelming; yet I hope there is mercy for the chief of sinners. I look again to the rock and refuge of my soul, and "other refuge have I none."[3] Lord, I turn unto thee with mourning and supplication; take away all thy wrath, and yet receive me graciously, and love me freely.

May 8, 1810 [Tuesday][4]
Last Monday at midnight[5] it pleased God to inflict, by means of a calculus passing the biliary duct, twelve hours of excruciating torture. A total obstruction of the functions of the stomach accompanied and increased the pain, and refused the strongest remedies: at length a warm bath (under a divine blessing) gave relief; but, together with the other applications, left me in a very reduced and languid state. At intervals of ease I had many solemn, interesting and, I trust, consolatory views of that state to which this renewed

---

[1] Hinton, *Biographical Portraiture*, 44.

[2] Isaac Watts, "My hope my portion and my God," stanza 2.

[3] Charles Wesley, "Jesus, Lover of my soul, let to thy bosom fly," stanza 2.

[4] Hinton, *Biographical Portraiture*, 84.

[5] May 1, 1810.

warning directs my attention. O may my divine Master but grant, that his name may be magnified in me, whether by my life or by my death!

June 3, 1810 [Sunday][6]

I am in my forty-ninth year. I have seen many changes, and the world is still full of them: O for faith to survey a better world, and grace to prepare me to enter thereon. I have not the solemnity I could wish for the Sabbath; but I trust God will increase it. A poor guilty condemned sinner I feel myself, but there is *one* in whom I hope I may say, I have Righteousness *and strength.* In this grace consists, and then glory shall follow. O what a miracle of mercy shall I be, if I reach the heavenly world! But with God nothing is impossible.[7]

... My subject is, "Peace I leave with you, my peace I give unto you:"[8] but oh what poor and unworthy ideas are mine on such a theme! O thou blessed Spirit, take of the things of Christ, and shew them unto my poor blind soul! And O grant that thy word, in my lips, may be like the five barley loaves, that multiplied in the hands of the disciples, and fed the people with enough and to spare!

---

[6] Hinton, *Biographical Portraiture*, 44–45, 119.

[7] Luke 1:37.

[8] John 14:27.

1813

February 23, 1810 [Tuesday][1]

I am without an assistant, and my spring complaints often prevent me from preaching. Our friends have written to Glasgow, to Mr. Kershaw,[2] as a supply in May and June.

---

[1] Hinton, *Biographical Portraiture*, 181.

[2] At this point Mr. Kershaw has not been identified.

1815

Not Dated, 1815[1]

The school is often the sepulchre of devotion; but it enables me in many ways to serve the cause which I love, and live (I trust) to promote.

My own feelings appear to be also those of my flock; many of them say that they have felt dulness, and hope for a revival. Lord, revive us again, that thy people may rejoice in thee!

[1] Hinton, *Biographical Portraiture*, 90–91, 200.

1818

February [?], 1818[1]

If it should please God to restore to me my dear friend, the comfort and solace of my life, I should be truly thankful; but whatever be the result, "It is the Lord."[2]

---

[1] Hinton, *Biographical Portraiture*, 84.

[2] On the illness of his wife, Ann.

1823

May 31, 1823 [Saturday][1]

This day closes the thirty-sixth year of my ministry in Oxford; all years of abundant goodness and mercy. I review them, I trust, with lively emotions of gratitude to my divine Master and Lord, who brought me hither, and has sustained me by his providence and his grace, through so long a series of arduous but delightful duties.

I entered this city, in compliance with the invitation of a small but spiritually minded church, June 1, 1787, an obscure individual, known to few, but directed by infinite wisdom. The call of this church was the first I ever received, and I never wished for another. Many others I have since received, but they had no attractions for me: with this church I began, and with it I hope to close, the ministry I have received from the Lord. Divine Redeemer, help me to fulfil it to the end!

My first three years I waited and hoped for success: the next seven the prayer of my heart was granted, and the church increased with the increase of God. In the tenth year of my ministry, antinomianism erected its standard, and collected some disciples, who disturbed my peace and threatened my removal; but this danger was mercifully dispelled, as it has been many times since, and I trust it always will be, for the sake of the church of my care, and of the general interests of divine truth in this vicinity. In my twelfth year, the increased congregation demanded, and God provided for them, a larger place of worship. The succeeding eight years were years of prosperity. My health and strength then declined for several years, beneath the weight of my labours: but kind assistance was granted,

[1] Hinton, *Biographical Portraiture*, 196–197.

through the ministry of my brethren Morgan,[2] Price,[3] Kershaw, and others; and the interest was kept from declining, though the uncertainty of pulpit supplies was sometimes injurious. In 1816, Mr. Thomas[4] was sent to my aid; eloquent, ardent, and popular. God knoweth, my whole soul rejoiced in that popularity ... "With my staff I passed over Jordan,"[5] and now I have many bands ... A church increased from twenty-nine to nearly two hundred members, with several branches from it; the meeting-house twice enlarged; and seven young men ... sent forth into the ministry. And still "the foundation standeth sure."[6] *Nil desperandum, Christo duce.*[7]

Not Dated, 1823[8]

This morning my friend, Mr.—, closed his christian race; and after a long season of great suffering, he, has entered, I doubt not, into the kingdom and joy of his Lord. Blessed be God, who has made my poor labours the means of his spiritual instruction and comfort. O may I labour with more zeal for those that remain!

---

[2] Thomas Morgan (1776–1857) was ordained on June 23, 1802, over the Baptist Church meeting in Cannon Street, Birmingham. On his ordination see Andrew Fuller and J[ohn] Sutcliff, *The Difficulties of the Christian Ministry, and the Means of surmounting them; with the Obedience of Churches to their Pastors explained and enforced* (Birmingham: J. Belcher, 1802). See also Hinton, *Biographical Portraiture*, 164, 197.

[3] Joseph Price (1769–1851) ministered at Alcester Baptist Church from 1815–1841, and then at Middleton Cheney, Northamptonshire, from 1842–1851. See Hinton, *Biographical Portraiture*, 179, 180, 181, 197. See also *The Baptist Magazine* 41 (January 1849): 33; *The Baptist Magazine* 44 (1852): 695.

[4] Jenkin Thomas (1793–1851) was pastor in Cheltenham and also co-pastored with Hinton in Oxford. Hinton, *Biographical Portraiture*, 186, 187, 193, 197.

[5] Genesis 32:10.

[6] 2 Timothy 2:19.

[7] Latin translation: Nothing is to be despaired of, if Christ is our leader.

[8] Hinton, *Biographical Portraiture*, 232–233.

This day I attended the funeral of Mr.—, one of my oldest hearers. I hope I was faithful to him; and I have some hope that he is safe, though he was certainly a very doubtful character.

Not dated

On His Dream[1]
If nothing remarkable in providence succeeds to this dream, I shall be surprised: yet I have no considerable dependence on it, but only wish that, by whatever means my thoughts are turned to this solemn subject, I may be induced more than ever to regard the sure word of prophecy, "and so to number my days as to apply my heart unto wisdom."[2]

On Usefulness[3]
My mind is much discouraged in my public work; I fear my usefulness declines.

I am surprised and thankful at the instances of success which God gives to my unworthy ministry.

[1] Hinton, *Biographical Portraiture*, 76.
[2] Psalm 90:12.
[3] Hinton, *Biographical Portraiture*, 122.

Appendix:

The Riot of Woodstock Narrative[1]

Early in the spring of the year 1794, I was requested by several of the inhabitants of Woodstock, some of whom had frequently heard me at Oxford, to preach to them at the house of Mr. [Thomas] Boulton, which was situated opposite the Malborough Arms Inn, in that town, and was duly registered for the purpose at the quarter sessions at Oxford. After many repetitions of this request, I agreed to give them a sermon as often as my other engagements would allow. Two or three other neighbouring ministers did the same; and the commencement of our labours was fixed for Sunday, May 18, on which day I was to preach. On the Monday preceding I went to Woodstock, and visited three families, who appeared to be worthy people; and I was informed that several other families were desirous of the worship of God among them, in the mode in which they had been used to enjoy it in other places, but of which they had been deprived since their residence there. Conceiving it right to forward their pious wishes, and having been quite unused to fear in the pursuit of my duty, I was rather surprised to find Mrs. Boulton uneasy at the clamours of some vulgar people, who had threatened to break the windows, &c. Having always found the laws of my country fully adequate to my protection, I had no doubt but they would be so in this instance. At once to remove, however, all uneasiness from my friends and all charge of imprudence from myself, I immediately waited on Henry Metcalfe, Esq. then Mayor of Woodstock, whose behaviour was such as I naturally expected from a gentleman and a magistrate: I claimed his protection for myself and the house, both

[1] Hinton, *Biographical Portraiture*, 255–261, 262–263, 265.

being qualified; and having particularly informed him of the time and place of our meeting, I received the pledge that there should be no disturbance. With this assurance I came home, very much satisfied; and on the ensuing Lord's-Day[2] I went to Woodstock, without any apprehension of danger, accompanied by my kind friend, Mr. Bartlett,[3] on horseback, while four other persons whose names are Hugh Barnard, Thomas Brock, Jeremiah Hooper York, and John King, went on foot. About a quarter past six in the evening the service commenced, very peaceably; the congregation consisting of about thirty persons, besides children, perhaps fifty in all.

After prayer and singing, I endeavoured to begin the sermon, taking for my text, Matt. xvi. 26. "For what is a man profited, if he gain the whole world and lose his own soul?" but at this instant a mob arrived, to the number of three or four hundred persons, one fourth of whom were Irish recruits. They were extremely noisy, and many of them began to rush into the house. With those who first came in I expostulated with apparent success; but a second set being more refractory, I spoke of the protection of the law, and the consequences of their breaking it, which last argument produced some effect on them also. Another and a more numerous company, however, still crowded the passage, armed with a well-pole and a scale-beam, which they thrust in among the hearers, using at the same time much abusive language. These implements were secured by

---

[2] May 25, 1794,

[3] John Bartlett (d.1823) was a deacon of Hinton's church in Oxford, and a member for forty-two years. In a letter written on his death, Hinton writes, "His attendance on the word and public ordinances was invariable, and he was one of the most constant at our prayer meetings, the devotions of which he frequently guided. Few christians have struggled with heavier afflictions, or borne them with greater fortitude. He was happy in training up a numerous family for God. Seven of them became members of this church, and the greater number of them preceded him to glory. Our loss by his death is great, but we are well persuaded his gain is far greater, and we know that Jesus, who ever lives, can supply every bereavement." Hinton, *Biographical Portraiture*, 192–193, cf. 24, 50, 132, 171, 172, 176 n., 253, 256, 258, 259, 264, 277 n.

some friends, and a little respite was gained, though it was of short duration. I attempted to go on with the discourse, but there were too many speakers for anyone to gain much attention. Some insulting language from persons in the room, and much noise and indecent behaviour on the outside of the window near which I stood, together with every symptom of increasing mischief, obliged me to break off the service and dismiss the congregation. I conceived that this step would have satisfied the mob, but they continued round the house, and their numbers appeared to increase: attended by two friends, therefore, I crossed the way to the Malborough Arms Inn, where I had previously taken tea. The moment I appeared the mob raised a prodigious clamour, by turns hissing, shouting, cursing, and vociferating "Jacobin rascal" with almost every possible expression of insult; and the other friends experienced the same treatment. When all had left the house, I still hoped the mob would disperse: but they gathered round the inn, and some of them even came into the room in which we were. I began now to be somewhat concerned.

A person was pointed out to me, whom some of my friends knew to be one of the Woodstock constables. I asked him if he was so, and he replied in the affirmative. I claimed his protection, but he positively refused it, because (as he said) he had "no order from the mayor." I therefore wrote a note, and sent it to the mayor, entreating him to interfere and suppress the riot; but the messenger brought an answer that gave me little hope of any speedy succour. Meanwhile the landlord and landlady were urging us to depart at one door, as the mob was pressing in at the other; and, indeed, there was no alternative. The friends on foot set out at the front door, while Mr. Bartlett and myself mounted at the back gate, closely followed by a most ill looking Irish recruit, who was armed with a short stick or bludgeon (as were also many others) and who, on our mounting, set up a terrible noise, which appeared to be the signal to his companions that we were going. At this instant we might have escaped by a back road, as we had good horses; but as our friends were gone the other way, we determined rather to share their fate than to leave them to the mercy of the mob, though we were not then apprehensive that they would be allowed, within a few yards of the mayor's house, and without interruption, to proceed to such dreadful outrages as we presently experienced.

Whilst we had been mounting and coming round the corner of a lane, closely followed by the above mentioned recruit, who cursed us more bitterly as we approached his companions, they had been shedding the blood of our friends. We saw a considerable quantity of it (and this was the first thing that truly alarmed me) lying on the stones in the street, and over it stood a middle-aged man, an inhabitant of Woodstock, swearing with all the fury of a demon. He first addressed me. "D— you," said he, pointing to the blood on the ground, "this is Jacobin blood, and yours shall go next."

"I hope my friends," said I, "they have not shed any one's blood."

"I tell you," said he, again swearing, "it is Jacobin blood, and yours will go next."

He repeated these words with additional ill language, to Mr. Bartlett, while multitudes all around him were uttering similar imprecations. At this instant a handful of dirt struck me on the left side of my head; I saw the man who threw it, who appeared to be a corporal: and at the same time the recruit who had followed us from the inn began most violently to beat the horses on which we rode. I attempted to run back, but in a moment, we were surrounded; every way of escape seemed closed, and all attempts equally perilous. The mob had now left pursuing our companions, and stones came thick upon us from all quarters. A stroke from a bludgeon totally disabled my right hand. I could however hold up my arm, which I did, and thus prevented repeated and violent blows (it is impossible to say how many) from reaching my head; but my arm was miserably bruised from my shoulder to my wrist. Having no alternative but death, we set ourselves to press through the mob towards Oxford. For this purpose we placed our horses abreast, and spurred them sharply; when, as though conscious of their situation, they reared and galloped with great force, but without in the least degree separating from each other, so that the rioters were compelled to fall back on each side of the road, and open a way for our advance. Everyone who could come near struck us with a bludgeon, or a stone, as we passed, and each of us was violently bruised on the side open to their assault; but one side of each being sheltered by the position of the other, we were enabled to maintain our seats and effect our escape.

When we had got a little before the mob, I discovered Mr. Barnard, who had just strength enough to crawl out of a ditch into which the cruel wretches had thrown him, having first so covered him with wounds and blood that he exhibited one of the most dismal spectacles I ever saw. Mr. Bartlett rode up to him, the rioters still pursuing at the distance of about two furlongs. "Barnard," said he, these "wretches have almost murdered you, and they are coming up again; but come, we will take you with us." The poor man was hardly capable of reply, for his speech was almost gone, and his senses seemed to waver; but he urged us to save ourselves, and leave him to a death which it seemed now impossible to avoid. "I will not leave you," said Mr. Bartlett: "if they kill you they shall kill me too. Come, be cheerful; 'tis a good cause, and we will die together." I rode up in the instant, and we contrived, though with great difficulty, to fasten his arms across the front of our saddles, and to drag him along between the horses. About three quarters of a mile from the town, the mob left us; and at the distance of a mile and a half we stopped, obtained some relief for Mr. Barnard, and waited for the rest of our companions, who had escaped by different roads, and were, all but one, severely wounded. With much gratitude to heaven that no life was lost, and with joy and tranquility of spirit which I have seldom felt, I assisted to bring home our friends, whose account on oath of what passed while we were separated, was as follows.

Immediately on their quitting the inn, the recruits and townspeople surrounded them and obstructed their way; and the soldiers endeavoured to enlist them, by forcing money into their pockets and coat sleeves. Expostulation was useless, and in truth did but increase their violence. Mr. Brock was almost brought to the ground by a blow between the shoulders; and perceiving one of them putting a shilling into his pocket, he pushed it away with his hand. This was highly resented by the recruits, who immediately laid on him in a most cruel manner; and he, perceiving that his life depended on his using the means of self-defence, exerted himself with so much energy as, after receiving many wounds, to affect his escape. Mr. Barnard was not so fortunate; being somewhat in years he was not able to make any resistance. By the force of many bludgeons striking at once, he was brought to the ground at least ten or twelve times successively, the mob just giving him time to rise, in order to have the brutal pleasure of knocking him down again. Deaf to all his entreaties for mercy, they at last threw him into a ditch, and while lying there one of them (he believes a sergeant) gave him several dreadful kicks on the ribs, and then called off the men. Mr. York likewise took his blows without resistance, but, being young and active, he escaped better than Barnard, who probably will retain the effects of his ill usage all his days... A warrant was obtained to apprehend some of the soldiers,[4] and intelligence having been received that they were to march through Oxford on the Wednesday following, I procured several constables to take the delinquents into custody as soon as they should be identified: but, on sending some persons to gain further information, we found that their number amounted to two hundred and sixty, and that they were entering the city with drawn swords, threatening destruction to all who should oppose them. The constables assured me that it was in vain to expect assistance in executing the warrant; that there were no officers who could exercise any control (there being none of a higher rank than sergeants); that many would join the soldiers; and that, in short, it was at the hazard of my life to approach the ranks to point out the culprits.

I scarcely need say that, with this intelligence, we were heartily glad to see them depart without doing us fresh injury: and I therefore returned the warrant to the magistrate, giving him the above reason for so doing, and intimating that, as justice might be obtained

---

[4] It could not be absolutely proved, that any persons but the soldiers were guilty of actual violence: but many of the inhabitants of Woodstock abetted the soldiers, and urged them on to the assault; and particular charges of this kind were exhibited on oath against several of them by name. —JH

in some other method, I chose rather to bear the injury for the present, than hazard the quiet of the city... I have never been eager for prosecution. I wish only protection; and if this be withheld I mean not to murmur, but to commit myself to him who judgeth righteously. Conscious of truth and integrity, I should have been happy to submit this cause to the most full and complete legal investigation: but though such an opportunity appears to be forever lost, I am not on that account discouraged. I shall the more attentively regard the advice of the sacred writer: "If thou seest the violent perverting of judgment and justice in a province, marvel not at the matter; for he that is higher than the highest regardeth, and there be higher than they."[5]

[5] Ecclesiastes 5:8.

Scripture Index

Old Testament

Genesis
32:10 79
Exodus
3:12 69
1 Samuel
3:18 47
1 Kings
18:12 27
Psalms
4:6 51
22:1 52
69:19 63
85:8 50
86:2 54
90:12 81
103:1 57
115:1 59
118:25 46
119:8 35
119:25 49
119:176 30
144:1 60
Proverbs
12:27 46
25:28 37
Ecclesiastes
5:8 89
Song of Songs
1:6 22
2:16 55
Isaiah
43:2 69
45:19 32
Jeremiah
8:22 36
45:5 23
Lamentations
3:22 55
3:25–26 52
Micah
7:19 48
Habakkuk
3:2 .... 35, 38

New Testament

Matthew
27:46 52
Luke
1:37 74
2:30 58
22:32 51
23:34 18
John
14:27 74
Acts
7:60 18
Romans
6:14 43
8:28 18
11:36 53
12:11 44
16:10 50
1 Corinthians
1:30 40
7:32 49
Ephesians
3:8 19
2 Timothy
2:19 79
Hebrews
6:12 44
13:8 .... 61, 65
1 Peter
1:8 53
3:7 58
5:5 21
5:7 23
1 John
1:7 24
Revelation
12:11 60
22:5 65

Date Completed	Name

H&E *Publishing*

www.HesedAndEmet.com

www.ingramcontent.com/pod-product-compliance
Lightning Source LLC
Chambersburg PA
CBHW021739190726
48288CB00009B/3111

* 9 7 8 1 9 8 9 1 7 4 5 1 7 *